PRAISE FOR

Enlightenment Is an Accident

"In an overly striving world, Zentetsu's message is refreshingly direct—spiritual discoveries come as accidents, and we'd best prepare to trip, stumble, and fall into the openness of mind. Full of wise humor and engaging stories, this book invites us into that surprising and delightful journey."
—Judith Simmer-Brown, author of *Dakini's Warm Breath*

"*Enlightenment Is an Accident* is a potent antidote to the materialism and bypassing on offer in many spiritual circles these days. Accessible and kind, Burkett invites us to take off our masks, see ourselves clearly, and welcome the accidents of life as the very ground of awakening."
—nico + devon hase, authors of *How Not to Be a Hot Mess*

"Tim Burkett's *Enlightenment Is an Accident* beautifully weaves stories from ancient wisdom, sixty years of Zen practice, and his time with some of the great planters of Buddhism on North American soil to create a warm-hearted invitation to a more joyous, more free, and kinder way of being in the world."
—Ben Connelly, author of *Inside Vasubandhu's Yogacara* and *Mindfulness and Intimacy*

ENLIGHTENMENT IS AN ACCIDENT

Ancient Wisdom
& Simple Practices
to Make You
Accident Prone

TIM BURKETT

Edited by Wanda Isle

SHAMBHALA

Shambhala Publications, Inc.
2129 13th Street
Boulder, Colorado 80302
www.shambhala.com

9 8 7 6 5 4 3 2 1

First Edition
Printed in the United States of America

Shambhala Publications makes every
effort to print on acid-free, recycled paper.
Shambhala Publications is distributed worldwide by
Penguin Random House, Inc., and its subsidiaries.

LIBRARY OF CONGRESS CATALOGING-IN-PUBLICATION DATA
Names: Burkett, Tim, author. | Isle, Wanda, editor.
Title: Enlightenment is an accident: ancient wisdom and simple practices
to make you accident prone / Tim Burkett; edited by Wanda Isle.
Description: Boulder: Shambhala, 2023. | Includes index.
Identifiers: LCCN 2022031763 | ISBN 9781645471356 (trade paperback)
Subjects: LCSH: Enlightenment (Zen Buddhism) | Spiritual life—Zen Buddhism.
| Meditation—Buddhism
Classification: LCC BQ9288 .B87 2023 | DDC 294.3/442—dc23/eng/20220713
LC record available at https://lccn.loc.gov/2022031763

Dedicated to those who aspire to
open up to
and live from a stillness unlimited
by space or time.

When you try to understand everything,
you will not understand anything.
The best way is to understand yourself,
and then you will understand everything.
—Suzuki Roshi

CONTENTS

Part Three

FALLING AWAKE

INTRODUCTION

Zen was introduced to the United States only a little over a century ago. Understandably, the philosophy and practice of Zen—both of which are quite foreign to the Western mind—are often misunderstood, even within the Zen community. As a first-generation American Zen teacher, I feel compelled to clarify some of the most misunderstood interpretations, beginning with a look at the ubiquitous idea of enlightenment.

After fifty-plus years on the Zen path, I've noticed that many of our most common and strongly held misconceptions can be traced back to the beginning, as we're struggling to find our way as new practitioners.

Part one of this book, Tripping over Enlightenment, covers this tumultuous and often confusing phase. This is the settling-in stage. We tend to flounder around a lot in the beginning, searching for just the right meditation center, with just the right aesthetics, the right membership, and of course, the right teacher.

The settling-in stage is much like window-shopping. You're on the outside looking in, asking yourself: *Is this the right place for me? Will I fit in here?* Good questions. A lifelong commitment shouldn't be taken lightly. It was an important part of my own journey, and I look back on it with both fondness and gratitude—along with a healthy dose of doubt that, fifty years later, continues to serve me well in practice and in everyday life.

As the contrarian approach of part one opens up small cracks in our conditioned mental and emotional infrastructure, a new understanding of reality begins to emerge. The Sanskrit word for seeing deeply into the true nature of things is *vidya*, which refers to a kind of awareness that penetrates delusion (*avidya*) and allows clarity and transparency to enter our consciousness. A committed vidya practice enables us to relax into whatever is happening and receive the wisdom and insight each moment offers. It also prepares us for the next phase of practice.

Part two, Stumbling toward Enlightenment, deals with the second, and the longest, phase of the journey: the revelation phase. This where the hard work of transformation begins.

The revelation phase focuses on the specific teachings and practices that offer glimpses into the interconnected nature of reality. It begins with one of the Buddha's early teachings, on what he called the five hindrances. But these primary energies hinder only so long as they operate below our radar. The Buddha's teaching reveals the underlying beliefs and emotions that sustain these five universal hindrances, allowing us to free ourselves from them.

Spiritual and emotional freedom sounds wonderful, but for most of us, the journey is filled with paradoxical assertions and confounding choices—like this one the Buddha presented to his followers. "What would you do if you came across a poison tree in the forest?" he asked his disciples, and then suggested three possible options: chop it down; put up a sign warning people away; or do the unimaginable and eat the berries.

Many teachings in the revelation phase may initially taste like poison berries in our mouth. When practiced with courage and sincerity, however, they reveal things about us that are unpleasant, often embarrassing, and occasionally traumatic. But these revelations are like signposts that mark the path. They show us our broken places so that we can welcome them back into our heart, nourish them with our kind awareness, and allow them to heal. If this book leaves you with only one takeaway, I hope it is this: the path to enlightenment leads directly through our broken places.

Stumbling toward Enlightenment offers teachings and practices that guide you through your broken places. For most practitioners, this phase of the journey is both disturbing and delightful as crusty old fixations dissolve and mind-expanding revelations begin to soften the boundaries that separate and divide—readying you for the last stage discussed in this book.

Part three, Falling Awake, is the embodiment phase. Here, embodiment means collapsing the dichotomy between right and wrong, suffering and joy, self and other. The advanced teachings in this third phase are understood on an intellectual level by many. Few, however, find meaningful ways to bring them into their daily practice.

When we do bring these advanced teachings into our regular practice, though, they have the potential to pull the rug out from under our conventional understanding of reality. Only then can we embody the richness and mystery of a thoroughly interconnected reality.

As the universal truths revealed in part three penetrate our flesh, blood, bones, and marrow, a nondual view of reality emerges. This third phase surfaces on its own, in its own time, and usually when we least expect it.

While it's true that every path to enlightenment is different, there are rhythms, similarities, and tendencies common to most, if not all. Together, these three phases prime the heart and mind for an inner journey that is often bewildering, frequently delightful, and occasionally euphoric.

The quote that became the title and theme of this book has been attributed to several teachers, including Suzuki Roshi and Aitken Roshi. However, it probably originated with Jiddu Krishnamurti, whose books I began reading during my first couple of years of Zen practice. Krishnamurti preceded any of the other teachers who've been credited as the originator. His original quote was, "Enlightenment is an accident, but some activities make you accident prone." Like most parables, folktales, myths, and quotes that have been around for a long time, it has gotten tweaked over time to its current form. So, though it has been embraced by many, no one teacher can take credit for its current rendition.

Regardless of its exact origins, the profound truth captured in these few words describes my Zen experience, from the morning in 1964 when I met Shunryu Suzuki until now, more than fifty years later.

Suzuki was my first teacher, and his voice resonates throughout this book. For me, he is as alive today as he was when we sat together at the San Francisco Zen Center. He lives on in my heart, and he speaks to me frequently in my dreams.

I hope you, too, will find a voice that lives in your heart and dreams, supporting you through difficulties, applauding your triumphs—and perhaps this book will help you find it.

TIM ZENTETSU BURKETT

PART ONE

TRIPPING OVER ENLIGHTENMENT

He who stands on tiptoe doesn't stand firm.
He who rushes ahead doesn't go far.
He who tries to shine dims his own light.
He who defines himself can't know who he really is.

—Tao Te Ching

1

SHOPPING FOR ENLIGHTENMENT

The first book I read on enlightenment was *The Teachings of the Mystics* by W. T. Stace. It was 1964. I was an undergrad at Stanford, and the book was research for my abnormal psychology class. After Stace's book, I moved on to Aldous Huxley's *The Doors of Perception,* in which he describes his life-changing psychedelic experience. Then there were books by Alan Watts and D. T. Suzuki. These books told stories of mystics from around the world having wonderful enlightenment experiences, which they described as being deeply calm and peaceful—and dynamic and ever-changing—all at the same time. *Can reality actually be this way?* I wondered. And yet, even with all my skepticism, I believed them. I'd even gotten a taste of it myself.

After reading the best books I could find, I moved on to trying to find the best Zen center. Searching under "Zen" in the San Francisco Bay Area phone book, I found two listings: the San Francisco Zen Center and the Zen Bar. I jotted down both numbers, just in case.

The Zen center (not the bar) led me to my first teacher, Suzuki Roshi. Moments after meeting him, I was infatuated—although he was not yet the idolized figure whose statue greets you as you enter San Francisco Zen Center today. (I think Suzuki would get a big laugh out of that statue.)

Sometime after I'd been practicing with Suzuki, I asked him to recommend other books. He shrugged, puzzled. "Why would you want to read a book? Just come sit with me every morning and every night."

Hmm. That didn't seem like much to go on.

All I had was Suzuki himself, and that was enough. He seemed to embody everything I longed for: the way he carried himself with lightness and grace and the way he seemed to have no personas—he was simply open and available. There was a presence about him that drew me in—I trusted him, despite my usual skepticism. I envisioned myself sitting effortlessly, as he did, in perfect posture and complete stillness.

But I didn't sit in perfect posture. I could barely even cross my legs. My mind was a chatterbox, my body shook during meditation, and my heart was filled with jealousy as I watched others sit perfectly for an entire meditation session.

Perhaps, I thought, what I need is a different teacher. After all, Suzuki's dharma talks were beginning to sound repetitive. His naturalness, which I had admired, was beginning to feel a little boring. And his Japanese accent was often difficult to understand. It seemed that the more I struggled with my own practice, the duller Suzuki's luster became. Before long, I began searching for another teacher.

I didn't have to search far. It turned out that the only other Zen teacher in Northern California lived just two blocks from the San Francisco Zen Center. His name was Tu Lun. And Tu Lun was a Chan master (*Zen*—both the word and the school itself—is derived from the Chinese *Chan*, itself derived from the Sanskrit *dhyana*, meaning "absorption" or "meditation").

Tu Lun's dharma name is Chan master Hsuan Hua. When

I met him in 1964, he was a complete unknown, but later he became a very important figure in Chan Buddhism, establishing several Buddhist institutions in the United States, including the Dharma Realm Buddhist Association with chapters around the world. In 1974, he founded the City of Ten Thousand Buddhas, one of the first Buddhist temples in the United States, located in Ukiah, California.

But when I met him, his Chan center was the living room of his small apartment. When I knocked on the door, he greeted me wearing a kind smile and a brilliant saffron robe. I was drawn to him immediately. He seemed to manifest the same naturalness and transparency that I'd sensed in Suzuki. He was a wellspring of spontaneity and unpredictability. And Tu Lun was definitely not boring. He was exciting—and kind of trippy.

Being Chinese, Tu Lun was very different from his Japanese counterpart. In China, he had lived in a cave and meditated for long hours, enduring long periods without food. He often told stories about wolves, which seemed to be his archetypal spirit guide. He showed us his scars from burning incense on his body.

He recounted a dreamtime experience he'd had while in the cave. During meditation, a wolf spoke to him and showed him images about coming to America. Tu Lun didn't know anything about the country, but the wolf told him there were people in the United States who were interested in learning about Chan. So he came.

When I looked at Tu Lun, it seemed that I was really seeing him—that there was nothing hidden, no face behind the face. No personas or masks. And this was San Francisco in the sixties where everyone seemed to have multiple personas—one for each occasion.

I yearned to put my own masks aside. They'd been a part of me for so very long, and sustaining them was exhausting. When

I asked Tu Lun about this, he suggested I meditate on the Chinese koan that asked: "What was your original face before your parents were born?"

I found this advice to be hopelessly confusing—and frustrating.

I was beginning to get that old feeling again. Tu Lun's luster was starting to fade, just as Suzuki's had. I'd heard all his stories—repeatedly. He didn't speak English, so every word had to go through a translator. And besides all that, I still couldn't sit in perfect posture nor quiet my chattering mind. My longing for the effortless grace I saw in both teachers was only increasing.

The more I compared my tumultuous inside to their calm and composed outside, the more difficult my Zen practice became. Instead of shedding my masks, they felt even heavier than before.

A MONKEY'S FACE WEARS A MONKEY'S MASK

> Year after year
> A monkey's face
> Wears a monkey's mask.
>
> —Basho, seventeenth century

Years ago, I had a friend whom I'll call Bob. He was a successful attorney, fiercely competitive and argumentative both at work and at home. In preparation for a family reunion, his wife talked to him about putting his best face forward—smiling more, being friendly toward everyone, and biting his tongue when he had the urge to argue or debate. Bob agreed to give it his best effort, and he did. But when he got home that evening, he was frustrated and exhausted.

Bob had developed his fiercely competitive persona during childhood and adolescence, enabling him to feel safe in a world that often seemed hostile. Bob isn't unique. In fact, we all get a lot of practice trying on and developing personas, adopting one mask and then swapping it for another, before even reaching puberty. A six-year-old can go from greedy to magnanimous or shy to performative within a single hour of play.

One of the first masks I remember wearing was given to me at a very young age. When I was four years old, my mother arranged for me to take an IQ test at the University of California in Berkeley where she had been a graduate student. When the results came back, she proudly announced to the world that I was a "gifted child." Getting that kind of attention felt wonderful. I wanted my parents to be proud of me. My mind immediately set about creating the perfect mask for a gifted child.

Year after year, reinforced by my parents, teachers, and even my peers, my gifted mask became the face I projected to the world. Like my friend Bob with his competitiveness, I got a lot from this persona. I was able to project confidence, competence, and authority. And, as with Bob, the mask solidified through years of conditioned learning and repetition.

So naturally, when I began my meditation practice, I proudly wore my gifted mask. After a while, however, as my awareness began to sense a constriction, the mask became heavier and heavier. It was quite unsettling.

Meeting Suzuki, and then Tu Lun, opened my eyes to a new world. Theirs was a world without masks—a world of openness, spontaneity, unpredictability, and ease. While I yearned for the naturalness that seemed to penetrate their entire being, I also recognized that the key to their natural ease was *freedom from yearning*. I was stuck in a catch-22.

NOW WEST OF THE RIVER, NOW SOUTH OF THE LAKE

Dongshan, a Chan master who lived in the ninth century, had been traveling for a long time, going from one monastery to another, from one teacher to another, before arriving at Yunmen's monastery.

"Where are you from?" Yunmen asked.

"From Sato," Dongshan replied.

"Where were you during the summer?" Yunmen asked, prying a little deeper. Was this monk standing before him shallow or deep?

"I was at the monastery of Hozu, south of the lake."

"When did you leave there?"

"On August 25," Dongshan replied.

"I spare you sixty blows," Yunmen said. It was a stinging rebuke.

The next day, Dongshan approached Yunmen and said, "Yesterday you said you spared me sixty blows. I beg to ask you, where was I at fault?"

"Oh, you rice bag!" shouted Yunmen. "What makes you wander about, now west of the river, now south of the lake?"

Finally, Dongshan understood. His eyes turned inward, and there he discovered his original face.

"Dongshan's Sixty Blows" is case 15 in the *Gateless Gate*, a centuries-old collection of Chan Buddhist koans. Intense koan work, which includes daily meditation and regular meetings with a teacher, can be mentally and emotionally exhausting. A devoted student may work with a single koan for weeks, months, or even years.

In addition to the story, most koans include a verse, usually written by a teacher a generation or two after the koan was recorded. Here's the accompanying verse for "Dongshan's Sixty Blows":

The lion had a secret to puzzle his cub;
The cub crouched, leaped, and dashed forward.
The second time, a casual move led to checkmate.
The first arrow was light, but the second went deep.

So what is "Dongshan's Sixty Blows" about? It's about the same thing that all koans are about: paradox. A koan creates a catch-22, a dilemma from which there is no escape. You are held there until the koan becomes an arrow that pierces the heart. All it takes is the smallest crack for the light to come in and resolve the koan.

There are many stories about monks who wander from place to place, and there are just as many about those who live in monasteries. Wandering is okay. Staying put is okay. After all his wandering, Dongshan went on to become a great teacher in his own right.

Whichever path you choose is the right one—*if* you stay with it until you realize that whether you are coming or going, walking or standing still, enlightenment happens when you make yourself available. Always, always, it happens on its own.

THE BEST MONASTERY

When Banzan was walking through a market he overheard a conversation between a butcher and his customer.

"Give me the best piece of meat you have," said the customer.
"Everything in my shop is the best," replied the butcher.
"You cannot find here any piece of meat that is not the best."
At these words Banzan awakened to reality as it is.

After practicing with Suzuki for about three and a half years, I began to consider going to Japan for an extended stay in a monastery. Suzuki was sending some of his senior students to Japan for months at a time, and I knew he was considering these students for ordination.

I wanted to be considered for ordination. One morning, I approached Suzuki and told him of my plans to go to Japan. I asked him about recommending a monastery for me. He thought I should go to Eiheiji, the famous Soto Zen training center where he had trained.

Eiheiji. Tourists went to Eiheiji. There was a lot of ritual there, and I wasn't good at ritual. Zen rituals are highly orchestrated; some almost like a dance. I was clumsy, and stumbling through a Zen ritual is a humiliating experience. I was not going to Eiheiji.

But Suzuki would talk only about Eiheiji. I started asking others to recommend a place. I talked to everyone I knew who'd been to Japan. For weeks, I read books and took notes. I wanted to find just the right place, one that best suited my ideal Zen practice.

One morning, as I was having breakfast with Suzuki in the kitchen of the Zen center, I eagerly laid out all I'd learned about the different monasteries. I'd narrowed down my search and was hoping he would help me select one of them. He listened attentively and nodded his head as I laid out the pros and cons of each one.

I finished and then waited patiently for his response. After several moments, I noticed that he seemed distracted. He was clearly looking past me. I followed his gaze to a shelf filled with raku teacups. These were among the few belongings he'd brought with him from Japan.

Still looking over my shoulder, he said, "If you try to find the best cup, Tim," he paused, his eyes gently meeting mine, "you will not appreciate any of them."

YOUR ORIGINAL FACE

If you reflect on your own true face, the secret will be found within yourself.

—Huineng

Huineng was born to a poor family in southeast China in the seventh century. His father, an administrator, died when Huineng was only three years old. For Huineng, school was not possible; as soon as he was big enough to wield an axe, he became a woodcutter to support the family.

One day, while at the marketplace selling wood, he heard someone reciting the Diamond Sutra. He was deeply moved; his insight into the profound teachings of this sutra ran deep. His entire life changed on the spot.

Shortly thereafter, he set out on a long journey to live and study at a monastery in northern China. Upon his arrival, Master Hong Ren recognized the great potential of this young illiterate and allowed him to stay.

However, since he could neither read nor write, Huineng was not allowed to study and practice with the monks. He was assigned to the rice-hulling shed. Even so, his insight was so profound that when Hong Ren was ready to retire and had to name his successor, he chose Huineng.

Knowing this would anger the monks who'd spent years meditating and studying sutras, Hong Ren passed his robe and bowls to Huineng in a secret ceremony under the cover of night. He then insisted that Huineng leave the monastery and go back home to Southern China.

When the monks learned of the secret ceremony, a group of them took chase, determined to bring back the robe and bowls that had been passed down through the five successors since

Bodhidharma, the first ancestor in the Zen lineage. The leader of the group was a monk named Ming. He caught up with Huineng on Taiyu Mountain.

As the angry Ming approached, Huineng laid the robe and bowls on a rock. "I will allow you to take them," he said.

But the robe and bowl were as immovable as the mountain. Realizing that the master was right to name Huineng the Sixth Patriarch, Ming asked him to share the secret of the Dharma.

"There is no secret," Huineng said. "Let go of your judgment about what is true and what is not and reflect on your own true face. The truth will be discovered where it abides—within you."

That was Huineng's first teaching as the Sixth Patriarch of Zen: The truth is discovered where it abides. Two centuries later, Yunmen said to Dongshan, "Oh, you rice bag! What makes you wander about, now west of the river, now south of the lake?" Eleven centuries after Yunmen, Suzuki Roshi was subtler: if you try to find the best cup, you won't appreciate any of them.

All three of these great teachers denounced the idea of a path leading us somewhere other than where we are right now. All three are telling us to reflect on our own true face. Enlightenment is not about traveling from here to there—it's about traveling from there to here. Right here.

When we let go of our judgment about what is true and what is not true and reflect on our own true face, we become less reactive to what others think. Less anxious and pretentious. More calm and open to the world. More authentic and sincere in practice and in everyday life. It's what we all want—and it's what the world needs.

We can set aside our masks and the false faces behind them, along with the limited, self-defeating, and self-sabotaging thoughts and ideas that drive us to search without instead of within. How silly we humans are to spend so much time and effort shopping around for our own original face.

A WARRIOR FINDS HIS ORIGINAL FACE

The warrior was just a young man when he was forced to fight against the Trojans. They shoved a bow into his hand and told him he was an archer. They fought for ten long years. When the war was finally over, he was no longer a young man, had no wife or family, and had never felt love in his heart.

He wandered around for months before he stumbled across a monastery where the monks were devoted to archery—not as means of war but as a spiritual practice to cultivate a calm heart and deep concentration. These monks were unlike anyone he had ever seen. After ten years of being surrounded by death and vulgar warriors, he yearned to experience the quiet calm of these priests. He begged the abbot to allow him to stay.

For ten years, the warrior lived with the monks. Then, when he had perfected his skill as an archer, the abbot said, "You have perfected your skill as an archer. There is nothing more we can do for you here." But the man's heart was still the heart of a warrior; he was not at peace.

He argued and pleaded with the abbot, "My heart is not at peace!" But the abbot would not change his mind. "What you are seeking is not here. Perhaps you will find it in the outside world."

He was older now, and felt older still, and once again found himself with no home and no family. His heart, which still had never felt love, became bitter. He became a swindler, tricking young arrogant archers to challenge him and taking their money when they lost.

After ten years swindling his way across the land, he came upon a forest that looked familiar, and then more familiar, and he discovered with surprise that he was very close to the village of his birth. He hardly remembered the place as he had been barely fifteen years old when he was forced to join Odysseus's army against the Trojans.

Walking through the surrounding forest, he noticed a bull's-eye on a tree with an arrow in the exact center. *Ah,* he thought, *another foolish archer will soon be parted from his coins.*

As he neared the village, he came across more and more trees with bull's-eyes and arrows in their centers. When he entered the village, he saw bull's-eyes with arrows dead center on the wall of the blacksmith's stable, the trading post, the feedstore, and even the church. There were bull's-eyes with a single arrow in the center on every wall of every establishment. *No one is so good that they hit the bull's-eye with a single arrow every time they shoot,* he thought angrily.

Growing more and more agitated, his warrior heart awakened. He would find this arrogant archer and take every coin he had. Quickly, he approached the elders of the town and demanded that the archer responsible for this perfection meet him the next morning in the forest where the river forked.

The next morning, he arrived as the sun was rising and waited for several hours, but no one came. Then he noticed a young girl playing by the river. Her clothes were tattered, her face smeared with dirt. *Just an orphan girl,* he thought.

"Are you waiting for someone?" she asked.

"Go away, orphan. I have nothing for you," he said, irritated.

"I cannot," she said. "I was told by the elders to meet someone here."

The man looked unbelievingly at the little girl and said, "I'm waiting for the master archer who shot perfect bull's-eyes all over the village."

"Well then, that is me," said the girl. On the ground next to her was a bow and a single arrow. She grabbed them up and walked toward the man.

The man, feeling more indignant still, looked skeptically at the girl. Finally he said, "If you are telling the truth, then explain to me how you can get a perfect shot every single time you shoot your arrow."

"That's easy," said the girl, brightening. "I take my arrow and I draw it back very tight in the bow. Then I point it very, very straight and let it go. Wherever it lands, I draw a bull's-eye."

At that, his frozen heart overflowed with warmth, peace, and love for the young orphan girl with the tattered dress and a single arrow. Laughing with joy, with tears in his eyes, he lifted the girl into the air and swung her around. "Come, let's go into the village and find a good home for an old man and his daughter."

2

IDIOT COMPASSION, EGOLESSNESS, AND OTHER TRAPPINGS OF ENLIGHTENMENT

Do not try to use what you learn from Buddhism to be a better Buddhist; use it to be a better whatever-you-already-are.

—The Dalai Lama

When we wall ourselves off from our negative feelings and emotions because they don't feel spiritual, we're missing out on the richest teachings Zen has to offer. Zen teaches us that enlightenment includes our broken places. Still, opening ourselves up to our broken places is difficult practice.

Refusing to face the things about ourselves that make us uncomfortable is called "spiritual bypassing," a term coined by Buddhist psychologist John Welwood, who is recognized for his work on the integration of psychological and spiritual concepts. I first heard the term in a class I took from him in about 1980.

According to Welwood, spiritual bypassing is "a tendency to use spiritual ideas and practices to sidestep or avoid facing unresolved emotional issues, psychological wounds, and unfinished developmental tasks."[1] So spiritual bypassing is a pretense that not only distances us from others, but also from ourselves. He goes on to say that spiritual bypassing is often a way of rationalizing our effort to "rise above the raw and messy side of our humanness before we have fully faced and made peace with it."

Most of us are guilty at one time or another of some type of spiritual bypassing, often without realizing it. Some cues may include feeling emotionally numb, indifferent, or aloof. Or maybe your internal tyrant tells you, over and over, that you shouldn't be thinking or feeling this or that. You may feel driven to express only positive sentiment, ignoring or pushing aside difficult emotions like anger or sadness.

There are times when anger is totally appropriate. There's a lot of energy in anger, which can be focused on making some big change within ourselves or a bad situation. And sadness is a deep emotional response that often brings us closer to ourselves and more compassionate to others. Spiritual maturity is about learning to experience all our emotions skillfully. Not acting on an emotion does not mean ignoring it.

If once-healthy relationships with parents, spouses, children, and close friends are falling apart because you are consumed with spiritual practice and/or the spiritual quest, this may be another cue that you are engaging in one or more spiritual bypassing behaviors. Let's remember that the personal and spiritual are not separate and it's beneficial to pay attention to what our negative emotions are trying to tell us.

Let's also notice when we are imprisoned by the constraints of a "spiritual superego," making spiritual teachings into prescriptions about what we should do, how we should think, how we should speak, or how we should feel. It's my deep belief that the only *shoulds* that are healthy are those that support our authenticity.

Our practice is strongest when we accept every part of ourselves, just as we are, allowing our most difficult emotions to become our deepest and most profound teachers. Radical acceptance of all our emotions naturally cultivates deep inner strength and compassion.

THE GOOD BUDDHIST

One of my role models early on was a homeless teenager. While many would come to the door of Zen Center with meekness signifying respect, and politely ring the doorbell, this young man would stand at the door and yell, "Open up!"

In my opinion, that's the spirit to have! Approach the sacred place with full self-respect, respect for your own sacredness, and demand to be let in—no slicing and dicing or fawning required! No arrogance either—just genuine commitment to your own basic goodness which is one of the foremost tenets of Buddhism.

—Jack Elias, "Zen and the Art of Spiritual Bypassing"

Too often, people doing a spiritual practice try to live up to some perceived idea about how a spiritual person should behave. To some that means being incessantly pleasant, always soft-spoken, politically correct, and through it all remaining calm and composed.

True compassion, however, is rooted in wisdom, not political correctness or social niceties. It is not sentimental, doesn't always look like compassion, nor does it always make you feel good. That's because it is not about you. And it's not about being liked or appreciated by others. It is about getting self-interest out of the way so you can respond appropriately to the suffering of others.

I get it. Being a do-gooder can feel very gratifying. But compassion is not about self-gratification. If you avoid confrontation when your gut is telling you something needs to be addressed but you fear how others may react, then it is not your spirituality at work. What's keeping you quiet is a combination of weak boundaries and a fragile ego. This is your conditioned self, not your authentic self. Authenticity requires courage.

When we are caught up in ideas about being a good Buddhist, we become exiled from our own natural, authentic nature. Zen is about realizing that everything permeates everything else—lit from within by same light.

Authenticity, when lit from within, allows us to get all the way down into the humus of our own existence. The good, bad, and the ugly are all right here in the humus, lit by the same light that permeates all that is and will ever be. Maybe the part of you that's always angry is the part of you that really cares. Maybe it's angry because it has something important to reveal to you, but you aren't listening.

Human beings came from the salt water of the oceans and from the richness of the soil. The fertile ground of the humus is aerated and moist because it's not separate from the air and rain. It supports us, but not in the way we're accustomed to think. It consists of all types of decomposing beings.

Suzuki Roshi said that waking up is a very simple process: it's a matter of caring for the soil. As we learn to live from the ground of our being, the bare ground with all matter of compost nourishing our practice, we can begin to experience openness, vulnerability, and authenticity.

Through our meditation practice we can discover the untended parts of our inner garden, the parts of ourselves that we have resisted. Only when we start tending these unwanted areas can we experience true compassion—as opposed to what Tibetan Buddhist teacher Chögyam Trungpa Rinpoche called "idiot compassion."

IDIOT COMPASSION

Idiot compassion is another symptom or form of spiritual bypassing. While a person may appear compassionate, it is more about their own needs rather than those of the receiver. Pema Chödrön, popular Buddhist teacher, author, and student of Chögyam Trungpa Rinpoche, says that idiot compassion refers to "the tendency to give people what they want because you can't bear to see them suffering."[2] It's also a common response when we just can't bear situations we ourselves find uncomfortable and we'd rather project suffering onto others than recognize and deal with our own discomfort.

Inherently unwise, idiot compassion doesn't consider the whole situation and, when supporting an already unhealthy situation, usually does more harm than good. It is the opposite of what recovery programs call tough love.

If you end up drained and exhausted from helping people, you're probably engaging in some form of idiot compassion due to weak boundaries. If your boundaries are weak, you may even experience someone else's pain as your own. It is important not to confuse weak boundaries with genuine compassion.

Another reason people engage in idiot compassion is to escape their own feelings of inadequacy. We should never underestimate the ego's need for recognition, especially for doing good deeds, as was the case in the following story about Emperor Wu and Bodhidharma.

TRIPPING OVER ICONS

Bodhidharma, the legendary fifth-century, cave-dwelling Indian monk who is credited with establishing the meditation (*dhyana*) school of Buddhism in China, was an intimidating figure often pictured with red hair, a red beard, and bulging eyes.

Emperor Wu, who considered himself a devout follower of the Buddha, devoted a lot of resources to promoting Buddhist temples, iconic relics, and silent meditation. The emperor wanted to be recognized by the great Bodhidharma for his contribution.

"What is the significance of all I have done?" asked Emperor Wu.

Bodhidharma growled, "No significance!" He saw clearly that the emperor, cut off from his own authentic self, was seeking validation.

Emperor Wu was confused. If his work to spread Buddhism with temples which featured rooms for meditation carried no significance, then where should he put his effort? "What is the fundamental principle of your holy teaching?" he asked.

"A vast emptiness with nothing holy about it," Bodhidharma responded.

Bodhidharma was pointing out a basic flaw in Emperor Wu's understanding of Buddhism. The direct experience of reality as it is unfolding has nothing to do with holy deeds, or even the concept of holiness.

Iconic describes something that symbolizes something else. Temples and holy relics symbolize the spiritual. Building Buddhist temples is a good deed, but it has nothing to do with the profound realization of reality. And much corruption has been hidden behind iconic images and concepts. Entering a holy place or touching a holy object gives us the impression that we are close to the raw power of the divine, which offers some feeling of security in an insecure world. But a direct experience with reality reveals that security is a delusion. If we want to experience clarity, we must accept the truth of insecurity. We live in a world that is ever-changing, and any fixed idea, concept, or ideal we're clinging to is a hindrance to our understanding. The Buddha said that one moment of clarity is better than a hundred years of delusion.

Zen master Yunmen, who lived about five hundred years after Bodhidharma, was one of the great teachers of his time and is often quoted in the record of Zen koans known as the *Gateless Gate*. Yunmen was even more direct than Bodhidharma when it came to freeing his followers from their dependency on religious symbols and icons. Here is case 21 in the *Gateless Gate*.

A student asked Yunmen, "What is Buddha?"
Yunmen replied, "Dried shit-wiping stick."

When religious icons and rituals support and deepen our spiritual practice, that's great. But too often, they get in the way. So more than a thousand years after Yunmen, we still need teachers to snap us back to an authentic Buddhist practice. The path to enlightenment begins after we break through our ideas about practice.

To know Buddha, we must move beyond ideas and judgments that trap us in an either/or view of life. Robert Aitken, a Zen teacher who gave me counsel when I visited him more than twenty-five years ago at his Zen center in Hawaii, wrote the following haiku while he was a prisoner of the Japanese during World War II.

In fermenting night soil
Fat, white maggots
Stream with Buddhahood.

Responding to Robert Aitken's poem, Zen teacher and author James Ishmael Ford wrote, "All of it, all of our lives are the stuff of our awakening. Even the shit. All the different kinds of shit. Our brokenness, our failures, our addictions. All of it, streaming with Buddhahood."[3]

THE EGO TRAP

> Don't lose actual practice for idealistic practice, trying to attain some kind of perfection.
>
> —Suzuki Roshi

Striving to free oneself from the delusion of separateness is what Zen practice is about. Zen is not about becoming egoless, abandoning our ego, or alienating, eradicating, or dissolving our ego. Zen emphasizes self-restraint, meditation, and the cultivation of mental clarity and emotional stability. Each of these practices requires a healthy ego. Besides, it's impossible to abandon our ego. Our individual conditioned self, our conscious self, is crucially important to both our well-being and our aspiration for enlightenment. When I got up at five this morning to meditate, as I do every morning, it was not my True Self that rolled out of bed, grumbling, with achy joints, scowl-faced, and groggy. It was my small self, which has trained for more than fifty years to get up at five a.m. to meditate.

So where does all the confusion about ego/egolessness come from?

The concept of ego came from Western psychology, not Buddhism. Ego refers to consciousness, more specifically, to the function of consciousness. Western Buddhist teachers began using the term *egolessness* to explain the Buddha's teaching on not-self; however, if we're going to use Western psychology as a kind of map of the Buddha's teachings, we have to make certain adjustments. Thanissaro Bhikkhu suggests that the Buddha's not-self teaching is not counseling egolessness; rather it is part of a regimen for developing a healthy ego.

Just as consciousness divides, separates, and reifies to make sense of the world, Western psychology divides, separates, and reifies consciousness for the same reason. Early Western psychology divided this separate sense of self (consciousness) into three categories: id, ego, superego.

Likewise, to make sense of our experience, early Buddhist psychology suggests that this separate self—often referred to as the small self or ego-self—is just a fabrication. This fabrication consists of a five-part process of internal experience, referred to as five "heaps" or aggregates: form, sensation/feeling, perception, concept, and consciousness, with consciousness being the one that dominates our lives as the storyteller (more on this in chapter 5).

But even in classical Western psychotherapy, the ego is not something to be annihilated because, in truth, *there's nothing to annihilate.* There is only a cluster of ego functions that are carried out in the mind. Often these ego functions work in opposition to each other. For example, an immature ego function may prod us to do something that will give us immediate gratification but lead to trouble in the long run, while a healthy ego function would nudge us toward activities that lead to long-term happiness and well-being.

Within traditional Asian cultures, particularly Japanese Zen culture, there's less emphasis on an autonomous ego and more on a group identity based on a sense of connection with family members, ancestors, and specific cultural norms. In that culture, a healthy ego is one that expresses our undivided nature rather than our individual nature. Here in the United States, however, the ideal is the go-it-alone type—the iconic figure of the isolated pioneer or cowboy. Here, the ideal state is one of independence, rather than interdependence.

In Zen, as in Western psychotherapy, the ego has no original existence. Therefore, ego is not an enduring function of reality; rather it is about our attachment to our ideals and views, including those that revolve around an enduring, isolated, independent self.

The Buddha saw himself as a wise friend who understood the nature of the ego and the possibility of liberation. He encouraged his followers to discover for themselves that ego arises from attachment, and liberation happens when we see deeply into our attachments and free ourselves from them.

STEPLADDER ZEN

My practice [when I was young] was what we call stepladder Zen: "I understand this much now, and next year," I thought, "I will understand a little bit more." That kind of practice doesn't make much sense—I could never be satisfied. If you try stepladder practice, maybe you too will realize that it is a mistake.

—Suzuki Roshi

Stepladder Zen is another trap many practitioners fall into. Suzuki warned us against becoming seduced by the idea that we will reach some pinnacle in the future. He referred to this future-leaning practice as stepladder Zen: today, I have this much wisdom, next month I will be wiser, and next year wiser still.

In stepladder Zen, we're always moving toward a goalpost and it's always somewhere in the future, just out of reach. This kind of practice creates a gap between you and the insight you seek. As Paul Simon said, it's always slip sliding away.

Then, as the future becomes the past, you may be looking over your shoulder and wondering, *Did I miss it? Did the promised wisdom pass me by? Is my practice good for nothing?* As Paul Simon wrote, "The information's unavailable to the mortal man."

You know the nearer your destination
The more you're slip slidin' away.
—Lyrics by Paul Simon

We cling so much to our hopes and dreams for the future—but the future is not the problem. How could it be? The future doesn't exist. Perhaps you're thinking, "But Tim, Buddhism is a *path*, isn't it?"

Yes, Buddhism is a path. But Zen is a dot—a dot that includes within it all the other dots. As you read these words in this moment, could this be the pinnacle? The dot reminds us that we can enjoy each activity by just giving ourselves completely to it, being totally absorbed in *this* moment, then *this* moment, then *this* one, on and on.

Zen practice is about full engagement in each moment. When our practice is wholehearted, each moment of practice is a moment of enlightenment, and each moment of enlightenment is a moment of practice. This means that the dot and the path are inseparable—to be on the dot is to be on the path. The dot is the pinnacle. The path is also the pinnacle.

So there's no need to wonder if you're on a path or on a dot. If you are a Zen Buddhist practitioner, the answer is yes. Yes to the path; yes to the dot.

This winding trail I'm walking now is leading me somewhere. It's a series of dots. I only have a dim vision of where I want to go, but that's fine. If my vision is too well-honed or specific, I may be captured by it and miss the joy of being present with each dot. Dot practice means embracing each moment fully without being caught by some ideal practice that will manifest in some imagined future. With no thought about past or future, staying on the dot is the path that always leads to the next dot.

When you're on a ladder, your focus is on the next rung. When you're on the dot, you are wholeheartedly engaged in the activity of that dot. The next dot emerges, and you discover that you're already there.

With dot practice, you learn to value both work (the path) and play (the dot) and experience that they are two sides of the same coin. If your work feels just like work, how can you make it more playful? Lewis Carroll has a suggestion in *Alice in Wonderland*:

> "No wise fish would go anywhere without a porpoise."
>> "Wouldn't it, really?" said Alice, in a tone of great surprise.
>
> "Of course not," said the Mock Turtle. "Why, if a fish came to me, and told me he was going on a journey, I should say 'With what porpoise?'"[4]

A playful porpoise as a metaphor for purpose is delightful. Yes, we all need a sense of purpose, but let's not be so intent on getting somewhere that we forget that play is as valuable as work, and more liberating.

Anything that is intrinsically motivated has a felt sense of liberation. It feels like we're being carried along. We may have a destination, but it's the process that is most valued. When my youngest grandson was four years old, he loved making sandcastles on the beach. His pleasure was not diminished when a wave came along and washed it away. Wholehearted engagement, not the result, was the source of his joy.

When you first come to Zen, it's difficult because you're looking forward to enlightenment and find no satisfaction in your practice. Inevitably, as your understanding deepens, you realize that kind of stepladder practice doesn't make sense.

> This is the secret of life—to be completely engaged with what you are doing in the here and now. And instead of calling it work, realize it's play.
>
> —Alan Watts

BEAUTIFUL SWAN OR UGLY DUCKLING

My Buddhist name is Zentetsu, which means "thorough-going Zen." It was given to me when I was ordained as a Zen priest in 1978 by my second teacher, Katagiri Roshi. But I also have another name that was given to me years earlier by Suzuki.

It happened during a two-month retreat at our Tassajara Monastery. I was sitting in a small room on a cushion, across from Suzuki. It was a one-to-one meeting that happened to be scheduled immediately after a long meditation session. My mind had become very still during that meditation, and I guess Suzuki could sense the stillness that I was experiencing.

His eyes twinkled as he leaned in and said, "You have become a beautiful swan."

I felt my face light up like the sun. I was a sun-faced Buddha! I felt so light I could have floated away.

Then Suzuki leaned back, scowled at me, and frowned. "Or maybe you are an ugly duckling!" And then he slapped his knee and laughed joyfully.

And so did I.

So that's how I got my first Buddhist name. Now, when I feel myself levitating off my cushion, I hear Suzuki's joyous laughter, and I am reminded of my own flawed and frail humanity. And that's okay. There's plenty of room for a befuddled and bedraggled little duck within thorough-going Zen.

3

THE LIBERATING PERILS
OF DEEP SEEING

A splendid branch issues forth from the old plum tree.
Thorns come forth at the same time.

—Keizan, Transmission of the Light

Enlightenment is about deep seeing and the splendid branches
that issue forth from deep seeing. These splendid branches—
mental clarity, emotional stability, and compassion—are the out-
growths of our practice and commitment. No matter how gnarled,
windswept, and wrinkled the old plum tree, new branches can
grow, and their plums remain delicious.

Deep seeing is about cracking open our psychological infrastructure and poking around in the deepest and darkest recesses of our being. But when you come through to the other
side, do not think you're safe from the thorns. For this would
only harden the heart and create calluses where the wounds
used to be, causing the old plum tree to grow brittle and no
longer bear fruit.

There's no getting around it—enlightenment is thorny busi-
ness. So let's just roll up our sleeves and embrace the process.

On one level, enlightenment is about discovering what it means to be human in an interconnected universe. On a deeper level, it is about discovering what it means to be an *interbeing*. Dogen Zenji, the father of Japanese Zen, said that discovering our interbeing nature, our Buddha-nature, begins by studying the self. In Zen, we study the self through a sustained meditation practice and regular meetings with a teacher. Of course, we start by studying our small self, our ego-self, because that's all we have access to in the beginning. As our meditation practice matures, however, and our small self is permeated through and through with awareness, it becomes a window into reality as it is, rather than how we perceive it to be.

The Sanskrit word *vidya*, which has the same root as the English word *vision*, is about seeing through the ego. An English translation for vidya is "deep seeing," but a more accurate translation may be "seeing into" or "seeing through" because vidya is about seeing through our delusions about space, time, and the existence of a separate, discrete self.

The potential to experience vidya is innate in all of us. It arises naturally and spontaneously when we are wholeheartedly immersed in *just* this moment.

Conversely, *avidya* is a fundamental blindness about reality. The core ignorance we call avidya isn't simply a lack of information; it is the inability to realize our interbeing nature. In Buddhist iconography, the key image of someone suffering from avidya is a person with an arrow in their eye. And, of course, we all suffer from arrows in our eyes. There's no escaping delusion. It's the human situation—we all suffer from it, again and again. In each moment, we are either manifesting our interconnected nature (vidya) or we're ignoring it (avidya).

Moving from avidya to vidya is a matter of penetrating the levels of awareness that overlay our natural ability to see clearly. The first is the level of ideas, images, memories, and evaluations. Here is where we spend most, if not all, of our time, squandering our attention on surface-level thinking.

Our emotional state is made up of a constellation of sensations and emotions, paired with our conditioned, instinctual drives. We all have instinctual urges that we're unaware of, yet they carry a tremendous force and drive. Below that is the level of our moods, which are subtler and more long-lasting. Often, we are unaware that our moods are influencing how we see the world.

Deep-seeing vidya creates cracks in this infrastructure, allowing us to look past these layers, along with the thought stream that sustains them and the feeling tones aroused by them. This kind of transparency allows the mind to slow down enough for clarity to break through.

THE PERILOUS WISDOM OF THE SHADOW

In the previous chapter, we looked at how walling off parts of ourselves can lead to practice pitfalls such as idiot compassion and spiritual bypassing. Such habits usually have deep roots, often in childhood. One of the major features of early childhood is the realization that some of our thoughts, feelings, and behaviors are acceptable, while others are not. Most of us, however, are not taught what to *do with* those aspects of ourselves that are unacceptable.

Deep inside our unconscious mind, a shadow self—those rejected aspects of our personality—is forming. Our shadow is composed of repressed ideas, instincts, impulses, weaknesses, desires, perversions, traumatic memories, embarrassing fears, and a myriad of small and large humiliations—whatever we don't want to admit having.

Many spiritual and religious organizations completely ignore or even condemn the darker elements such as anger, vengeance, control, shame, competitiveness, jealousy, and lust as evil. This is the birthplace of the fear body, which buries these negative emotions deep inside of us. And while this happens naturally through the acculturation process, if it is not attended to wisely, it can have perilous consequences.

Rejected aspects of our personality do not vanish; they become a shadow personality. And each rejected aspect within our shadow carries within it the seed of wisdom; it is waiting to show us something important about ourselves. But this feels quite perilous as it requires us to see things we don't want to see, accept the unacceptable, and embrace the deplorable. The wisdom of the shadow is about manifesting wholeness and balance—what Dogen called whole-being Buddha-nature.

Shadow wisdom emerges through cultivating the deepest aspects of vidya. When we acknowledge our repressed anger and traumatic memories and follow each all the way to its roots, we learn to set better boundaries for ourselves and others. If we acknowledge our sadness and have the courage to feel it with our whole body and mind, we cultivate the ability to experience the deepest and most profound joy. Shadow wisdom reveals the secret to abiding happiness: the realization that when we limit the expression of one side of our emotional spectrum, the other side is equally limited.

Shadow wisdom cultivates authentic compassion that arises spontaneously. When we're able to accept our own frailties, we are then able to extend the same compassion to others.

KARMIC KNOTS, DRUNKEN MONKEYS, AND GETTING RID OF BUDDHA

The trappings of enlightenment have dogged mainstream American Zen converts since its inception in the sixties. It's important to examine the many junctures along the way where we are most vulnerable to these pitfalls.

Once I finally settled on a Zen center and a teacher, I no longer struggled so much with ego or clung so tightly to my ideals. I began to experience some moments of real calmness and, eventually, realized that I could remain calm regardless of what was going on. As my concentration stabilized and I was able to stay with my breath for longer periods, I became more confident in my ability to do this practice. Even my posture improved. My mind still chattered, of course, but it didn't dominate quite so much. I felt lighter, less burdened, and more comfortable on and off the cushion. This, I soon discovered, was just the beginning of a genuine meditation practice.

An authentic Zen practice begins when we start to peel the onion, to bring the fresh air of awareness into the fears, resentments, and traumas that have hardened our heart. We don't choose to move into this difficult stage of practice; it happens on its own as a sense of separation and loneliness starts seeping into our awareness. Comfort vanishes. Anxiety bubbles up, and we begin to experience more psychic pain than we had before.

Some students blame the teacher, or the Zen center, and revert back to the shopping stage, which is unfortunate because the work of peeling the onion is crucial to our growth as Zen practitioners, as well as maturing human beings.

This transformative stage is always marked by difficulty. It can even be disorienting. It *should be* disorienting so we can reorient to a self that does not revolve around the ego. I was reminded of this in a most unlikely place: my drama class at Stanford. I complained to the teacher about the despicable characters he kept assigning to me. He said, "Tim, I thought you were a spiritual seeker. Don't you realize that you can never really achieve liberation until you have explored the deepest and darkest recesses of your being?"

As long as we cling to a narrow view of calmness or even enlightenment where everything is pleasant and comfortable, we have not yet fully committed to a vidya practice. Feeling our pain is essential, but when we feel it with our kind attention and with compassion, we do not suffer. In vidya practice, we learn how to relax into whatever is happening, even our pain. We relax and release, over and over. With each release, our insight deepens.

Opening up to the karmic knots of the past, those painful wounds we've been carrying around for years—or even decades—is difficult work, so we must always be gentle. I recommend a practice that I've found to be effective that I call turtle practice. Have you seen how a turtle protects itself by pulling its entire body into its shell? Shining our light of awareness in this practice is a similar simple and gentle process. Start by drawing all of your kind attention inward. Your kind, gentle, nonjudgmental awareness is all the protection you need as you do this deep exploration, which brings with it space for not only deconstruction but the reconstruction that follows.

As we do this, it becomes easier to remain open not only to what's happening in our head but also to the feeling tone associated with each of our thoughts. Old wounds get lodged in the body. If we cling to our old stories about those wounds—reliving, over and over, what happened and who's to blame—our awareness remains shallow and never gets down to the subtle level of feeling tone and bodily sensations.

The human mind is being filled with drunken monkeys, jumping around, screeching, chattering, carrying on endlessly.

—The Buddha

Perhaps this is where the phrase *monkey mind* came from. Our thoughts jump around like drunken monkeys leaping from tree to tree. But that's okay. As long as you keep moving your focus away from your thoughts and into your body, becoming aware of the sensations that are always arising, you don't have to worry about drunken monkeys sabotaging your efforts to meditate. Quite naturally, your heart begins to open to old wounds and other karmic knots of the past.

It's my experience that our most troublesome karmic knots are those that arise from childhood trauma, shame, and anger. We all have some degree of difficulty from these three entanglements. Through our meditation practice we can gradually experience an unwinding that allows whatever difficult experience we have to complete itself. Beginning with trauma, let's see how we might unwind each of these primary karmic knots.

Trauma

Life hurts all of us, and we all carry old wounds. Whether these wounds are rooted in childhood traumas, sexual violence, or racial injustice, the question is how to deal with them. Openness and nonjudgmental attention to these wounds lead to strength and wholeness, regardless of how deep and severe the wound.

If we don't acknowledge our traumas and make peace with them, they will continue to trip us up—in our practice and in our lives. It's important to recognize that making peace with deep and severe wounds is not easy and may require professional intervention along with your meditation practice. In an article titled "What Meditation Can't Cure," psychotherapist Debra Flics explains how meditation and therapy work together to heal deep wounds: "As painful thoughts and feelings emerge in treatment, a meditator will initially be more likely than a non-meditator to understand that thoughts and feelings are internal phenomena that do not have to be acted on."[5] Often, the first step toward healing is disempowering trauma-induced thoughts and feelings so they can no longer bully us into harmful actions.

Once a safe mental and emotional environment is established, a committed meditation practice allows us to develop a healthy relationship with our internal processes. No matter how long you've been meditating, a traumatic memory may surface at any time. When it first presents itself, your feelings may not be clear. But since all emotions are held in the body, staying with your bodily sensations is the key to untangling those karmic knots.

As we discover our capacity to open our heart to whatever arises during meditation, we may even find inspiration from unwinding the karmic knots that hold old traumas in place.

Shame

If we feel ashamed of something as adults, whether we are consciously aware of it or not, it is most likely evoked by a childhood memory. Maybe you didn't know the answers when called on in class, or maybe the person you were attracted to rejected you. Maybe you were teased or bullied for your size, weight, or the way you dressed, or maybe, like me, you were the last one chosen to be on a team.

The shame we feel today may catapult us right back to the rawness we felt then. We may feel off-balance, unworthy, or simply want to hide, just as we did then. Shame damages our image of ourselves in ways that no other emotion can, causing us to feel flawed, inferior, worthless, even unlovable. Shame is a response to helplessness and the indignity suffered. Often, we take personally what is actually quite impersonal. Whatever happened in the past arose out of a complex series of causes and conditions over which we had little or no control. Recognizing and acknowledging shame, rather than denying or avoiding it, is the first step. When we start to feel depleted, inferior, not good enough, or defective, shame may be kicking in. And we can learn to recognize its energy. Unfortunately, when it does arise, we often build up a wall of shame denial. This wall can include refusing to acknowledge our own mistakes, being hypercritical of others, or dumping on others in some other way. The more we think we need to be perfect, the more likely we're being driven by the energy of shame.

Even though shame—together with the fear that comes with it—creates powerful karmic knots, this doesn't have to be a problem. It only plagues us if we repress it, try to wish it away, or let it hold us back from doing what we want to do. Shame commonly manifests in one of two ways: withdrawal/disengagement or enmeshment/going along to get along. A powerful meditative technique for healing shame is turtle practice. When you gently draw your attention inward and shine the light of your kind, gentle, nonjudgmental awareness on the feeling tone of shame, it can heal the wounds created by some childhood trauma.

Modern research on the human brain's neural plasticity has proven its capacity to grow new neurons and make new synaptic connections. This means that it's possible to pair the old shame memory with new experiences of self-empathy and self-compassion. When we do this, we are re-pairing!

When we face shame and its effects on our lives, our wounds do not disappear. But through self-awareness and self-compassion, the shame no longer has the capacity to imprison our heart and mind.

Anger

In addition to recognizing how conditioning can affect our lives, it's important to recognize the power of our emotions. In Buddhism we talk about wholesome emotions and unwholesome emotions, and we emphasize that emotion tends to drive our lives. Although the idea of emotion driving your life sounds negative, it can also be positive.

In American culture, it seems that anger is one of the most prevalent of our strong emotions, or at least it's the one that causes the most trouble. Pent-up anger is usually rooted in insecurity and manifests as the need to succeed, to dominate, to feel loved and valued.

On an evolutionary scale, anger is a mechanism of survival. When we feel threatened, anger is our body's natural defense system. Our body is flooded with adrenaline. Without anger, humans probably wouldn't have survived in a world filled with predators.

Anger is also used as a powerful tool to manipulate or intimidate others in order to get what you want. People pay attention when we become angry. But we don't realize how addictive anger can be. It can control our lives.

So how do we work with anger in a way that it doesn't become a loaded weapon pointed at ourselves or our loved ones? First, we must listen to what it has to tell us, because anger is also information. In the same way that physical pain informs us about our body so we can take care of it, anger informs us that our mind and heart are in pain. Viewed in this light, anger becomes an opportunity to change and grow. However, our conditioned reactivity to anger is always a problem. Conditioned reactivity, when triggered, has the power to turn our mind off and the adrenaline faucet on—a very destructive situation.

We all have seeds stored in our unconscious. By the time you get to my age, you'll likely have a lot of them. But that's not bad. They are the calcification of emotional memories that are lodged within. They become activated when monkey mind draws on their content, but we can develop the capacity to work with seeds of anger, sadness, and other emotions skillfully as they arise. Over the years, I've supported many practitioners in this process. Here's an example.

Bill had a committed daily meditation practice, but when he finally engaged in retreats as well, a few unexpected emotional responses were triggered. As he sat facing the wall, hour after hour, he began to feel irritated by little things. Particularly, the labored breathing sound coming from the person next to him.

In his one-to-one meeting with me, he said he felt trapped and angry in the same way he had felt growing up when his father forced him to do chores on weekends instead of being with his friends. I encouraged him to hold that anger with kind and gentle attentiveness and curiosity, neither indulging it nor suppressing it, and see where it led. Several days later, he reported that the anger had turned into sadness about the friendships he'd missed because of his father.

Once Bill was able to fully tap into this sadness and embrace it with his kind attention, he began to experience a spaciousness around it, and within that spaciousness, a feeling of tenderheartedness arose, even for the person next to him who was "breathing like a steam engine."

We can each develop a tender relationship with whatever arises during meditation. As with Bill, this may heighten our sense of intimacy with the deepest part of ourselves—and with those around us. Anger arises for a reason from our karmic past, so our practice is to shine the light of awareness on it when it does. The capacity to see our anger clearly as it arises and be with it in kindness is enlightened activity. As long as we have seeds of anger stored in our unconscious, the possibility to actualize enlightenment is here.

The key to reeling in our problematic emotions is to hold them in our kind and gentle awareness without feeding them with our stories. In meditation, we learn to recognize the feeling tone of each emotion and sense where it is held in our body. We become aware of the intensity of it and begin to see our reactive patterns when a pent-up emotion is triggered.

Cultivating the ability to skillfully release our strong emotions is important because as old karmic knots are dissolved, new ones are constantly being formed by our beliefs and ideals. Liberating ourselves from these beliefs and ideals, including our beliefs about what it means to be a Buddhist, is what Zen is all about. Only then are we able to live authentically in this moment.

The Perilous Teachings of an Iconoclast

If you want an intimate understanding of enlightenment, you should get rid of you and Buddha.

—Keizan, Transmission of the Light

The second-century, semimythical lay teacher Vimalakirti stood out as an unrelenting critic of spiritual pretension. According to Vimalakirti, any attachments to dharma practice were not the true Dharma.

In a time when the spiritual path was marked by a rejection of material wealth, Vimalakirti, a devoted follower of the Buddha, was a rich man. And he was unapologetic about his wealth. He is often depicted wearing a large white hat and a flowing white robe made of the finest fabric. His wife, son, and harem lived in luxury, with a staff of servants to take care of their every need.

At a time when monks lived in monasteries, Vimalakirti was openly critical of the monastic life, choosing instead to remain thoroughly engaged in the world, without regard to class or social status. He was a familiar and celebrated figure in taverns, gambling dens, brothels, and social clubs for the rich and powerful. And yet, he is so important to Mahayana Buddhism, which includes Zen, that his story is told in a sutra named after him. And his teachings are among the most popular to Zen practitioners around the world.

Vimalakirti used his great wealth to help the impoverished. Although he had a wife, a son, a harem, and servants, he abstained from all sensual indulgence. Although he frequented the upper-class financial exchanges and engaged in trade, he was uninterested in personal profit. Zen teacher and scholar Taigen Dan Leighton writes, "Vimalakirti's teachings centered around his belief that we can only awaken in the context of intimate contact and involvement with the follies and passions of the world."[6]

Although Vimalakirti's story feels a little like having your cake and eating it too, the sutra is about seeing through the trappings of spiritual life. Its focus is on the inadequacy of isolating yourself from the ordinary world while surrounding yourself with sacred scriptures and religious symbols.

The iconoclastic wisdom of Vimalakirti espoused total immersion in the deluded world. Only within the deluded world can we learn to recognize our own shadow self and cultivate the courage to embrace it. Only when immersed in the deluded world can we cultivate genuine compassion for those struggling all around us.

THE HEART ATTACK SUTRA: THE DESTRUCTIVE NATURE OF ENLIGHTENMENT

Penetrate the true meaning of the Heart Sūtra,
and nothing will be the same again.

—*The Heart Attack Sūtra* by Karl Brunnhölzl

Another sutra that gets right to the heart of the matter is the Heart Sutra, which is chanted every morning at most Zen centers and Tibetan temples throughout the world. This sutra does such a good job of getting rid of both you and Buddha that it has been called the Heart Attack Sutra—as it seems to deny the validity of the Buddha's fundamental teachings.

According to the myth, the Heart Sutra was among several of the Buddha's advanced teachings that were discovered five hundred years after his death. When monks heard this radical teaching for the first time, so the story goes, several of them dropped dead from a heart attack.

Although practiced by other Mahayana schools as well, the Heart Sutra is the scripture most closely associated with Zen. The teachings within it cut through our conceptual framework, including our ideas and beliefs about spiritual practice. And they do so on a fundamental level, leaving absolutely nothing intact, nothing for us to cling to.

I was often frustrated by Suzuki's reluctance to explain the Heart Sutra. We chanted it every day after meditation. Containing phrases like, "form is emptiness; emptiness is form," it negates everything that exists in the ordinary world: "no eyes, no nose, no object of sight, no object of mind."

I told him once that I had some college buddies who were interested in meditation. I had invited them to join us for the morning sitting, and they were planning to come. My concern was the Heart Sutra—I knew we would chant it together, and I didn't want my friends to think I belonged to some crazy cult. Would he explain it to me so I could answer the questions my friends were sure to ask?

"Yes," Suzuki said. "But let's do it later. Look at all the sweeping we have to do. Help me with the sweeping first."

We did the sweeping. Then he was off doing something else. It seemed he'd forgotten. The same thing happened again for a second time, only then he had to wash the dishes first. The last time I asked was in Palo Alto at a sitting group. The difference was my buddies were actually there. "Well, can we talk a little bit about the sutra we just chanted?" I suggested eagerly. "Oh, I promised Darlene we would work on the trees in her yard. They need pruning, and I was hoping you boys would help me prune them." So we all went to Darlene's house and pruned the trees.

Back then, I had little interest in sweeping floors, washing dishes, or pruning trees. But I did have a deep desire to disabuse my Stanford friends of their skepticism about this Zen stuff. I wanted to talk to them intelligently about my practice—ego always wants to measure and analyze and present itself well.

Suzuki never did explain the Heart Sutra to me, but I've come to a relationship with it after years of chanting and studying it. In its deepest sense, the Heart Sutra is a sword that cuts through all we hold dear so we can experience the world directly, with no self-involvement. I finally realized that we don't chant the Heart Sutra to understand it. We chant it to imbibe it.

The radical message of the Heart Sūtra
is a sweeping attack on everything we hold most dear:
our troubles, the world as we know it,
even the teachings of the Buddha himself.
—Karl Brunnhölzl

PART TWO

STUMBLING TOWARD ENLIGHTENMENT

If you chase after it, you will stumble over it.
If you don't chase after it, your practice will decline.
If you chase after it, your effort separates you from it.
If you don't chase after it, you'll never discover that
there's nothing to chase after.

4

FROM PERILS TO PORTALS
Befriending the Hindrances

"How can I mature spiritually and emotionally without losing myself in the process?" This question, in one form or another, comes up frequently in my one-to-one meetings with Zen practitioners. Typically, it stems from some unconscious beliefs, passed down through family and culture, about how a spiritual person should comport themselves, as if there's a one-size-fits-all mold. We are rarely aware of how these unchallenged ideals impact our efforts to live an authentic life, which is exactly what the spiritual path is about. We are spiritual beings by nature, and the spiritual path is that which leads us back to our authentic self.

When we open up through the center of our own personal weaknesses and limitations—when our practice is to see ourselves clearly, without judgment or denial, and then work outward from that core—we do not lose ourselves in pretense or posturing. Buddhism has long appreciated the importance of working with our frailties and weaknesses. The ancient teaching of the five hindrances helps us recognize them as they arise so we can manage them skillfully.

The five hindrances refer to primary energies that we all struggle with throughout our lives, regardless of how many enlightenment experiences we may have experienced. They are: (1) craving and greed; (2) aversion, anger, hatred; (3) lethargy, apathy, boredom; (4) restlessness and worry; (5) doubt. We can use these mental and emotional energies as a kind of psychological map that takes us deeply into our own conditioned psyche. Working outward from there creates the possibility for our authentic self to emerge quite naturally.

The Buddha likened the hindrances to a poison tree. If we stumble across a poison tree in the forest, he suggested we have three options. First, we can try to kill it by chopping it down (typical of the Western mindset). Another option is to put up a sign that says, "This is a poison tree. Don't eat the berries, don't eat the leaves." This option allows us to take shade under it. Or we can choose the third option: We can say, "Oh, a poison tree, just what I've been looking for. These berries make the best medicine for curing many illnesses, including the illness of desire, aversion, sloth, restlessness, and doubt. I'll take these difficult energies and distill them in my own body and heart until I have converted them into medicine to support my life."

Learning to work with the hindrances, embracing and transforming them, may very well transform a life of pretense and posturing into one of authenticity, deep joy, and genuine compassion for ourselves and others.

HINDRANCE ONE: CRAVING AND GREED

The first hindrance includes both physical cravings, such as food, comfort, and sex, and emotional cravings, like being recognized by others, feeling loved, and yearning for fame and notoriety. Craving, in whatever form it takes, is about immediate gratification. Often, it is our emotional cravings, driven by a fundamental insecurity about our identity or place in the world, that give us the most trouble.

In my early days of Zen practice, I watched my friends imitate Suzuki Roshi. They shaved their heads, wore only black as he did, and even imitated his speech patterns, including the grammatical mistakes typical of those for whom English isn't their first language. Driven by insecurity and a craving to embody Buddhist teachings the way Suzuki did, they resorted to an awkward and ineffective fake-it-till-you-make-it approach to Zen.

When we are thrown off-balance by a particular craving, how can we work with that energy? Instead of repressing, resisting, or indulging it, we can use it to cultivate vidya. As we learn to recognize it as it arises, as it peaks, and then as it dissolves, it loses its power over us. This is the path to an authentic meditation practice.

For example, I love chocolate. In fact, I would say my craving for chocolate is almost insatiable. But instead of reaching for it immediately, I stop to feel the actual sensation of craving in my body. I become aware of the tension and pain that wax and wane with the intensity of the craving. Then, I notice how quickly the tension and pain dissipate as the chocolate touches my tongue and melts in my mouth.

What great happiness that first bite brings! But how much of this happiness is about the chocolate and how much is about getting some relief from the tension and pain associated with craving? And of course, we all know what happens when we feed a craving: next time, the craving pain will be more intense, and our resistance brittler.

Often, we don't even realize that the emotion we are experiencing—whether it's anger, confusion, sadness, or hatred—is emanating from the craving itself. The object of the craving is a crafty misdirect. As soon as one craving is fulfilled, another is already in the pipeline.

By looking closely at the emotion and recognizing how it intensifies, what thoughts come up, and the physiological changes that occur, we may be able to track the origins of the emotion back to its root. In Buddhist meditation, this type of investigation is called *skillful means.*

When we're able to manage our cravings skillfully, we avoid the danger of being overwhelmed by them. We're not avoiding the emotion; instead, we experience the sensation of each phase—the arising, the peak, and then its dissipation—without judgment. By studying our cravings in this way, we may get a better understanding of why they arise in the first place and how they affect our relationships with family, friends, and colleagues—both when we get what we want and when we don't.

As a first child, the former CEO of a large nonprofit agency, and guiding teacher at the Zen center for nearly two decades, I am used to people following my direction. I also have a strong desire to be right. I love to be right. It feels good to be right and have everyone follow me along. But how do you think my wife responds to my strong desire to be right? More than once, she has reminded me, "You're not my CEO!"

After more than fifty years of meditation, this can still be a powerful trigger for me, even coming from my wife. At times, I'm able to notice my immediate resistance, feel the tension in my body, and realize that it's my ego-self that feels threatened—the self built around the story that people should follow my direction. Then I can just chuckle at myself. Other times, I've acted out that story before I know what I'm doing!

Through skillful means, we can relate to each of our cravings in a friendly, compassionate, and wise way by focusing not on the object of desire but the actual sensation, which includes the pain or fear that evoked it. It takes courage to do this. It also takes a regular meditation practice to slow down our reactivity enough that we can really pay attention. It is very important to note that this is not punishing or heavy-handed work. A key component of skillful means is lightheartedness.

The Dalai Lama, speaking at Gethsemane Monastery, said that he had just been given a piece of cheese and he really wanted cake. His reaction? He guffawed. When we simply allow ourselves to experience the feeling that lies behind our craving, it loses its power and, like the Dalai Lama, we can just laugh!

It is important to note that the first hindrance is not about rejecting desire. To be human is to experience desire. However, even when the desire is positive and appropriate, if we cling to it and contract around it, it becomes a craving. If we notice that a positive desire is becoming harmful, we can focus on its impermanent nature. We can remind ourselves that everything is always changing.

The Buddha acknowledged that desire can be healthy and is not always to be denied. Speaking with his son, he said, "Rahula, if your desire will lead to harmful consequences for yourself or others, you must not act on it. If, upon close investigation, you see no harmful consequences, you should enjoy the fulfillment of your desire, and allow that joy to nourish your practice."

HINDRANCE TWO: AVERSION, ANGER, AND HATRED

For four years, Angela maintained a committed and diligent meditation practice. Recently, in a one-to-one meeting, she said, "I shouldn't be confused after all this time. Can you help me with this?"

I replied, "Every time you hear that voice saying you're not doing it right or you should do more, or whatever, count the judgments for a while, just to see them."

At our next meeting she said the problem had not abated.

"Alright," I said. "Continue counting them, but this time give thanks with each count whether you feel thankful or not."

The next time I met with Angela, she was still experiencing confusion. But she was much more relaxed and accepting of her practice—which included recognizing both her confusion and her aversion to the confusion. The confusion was not the problem. Her aversion to the confusion prevented her from embracing what was happening and transforming the energy.

As I wrote this story about Angela, I was returning from a visit with my grandsons, who live in Paris. At the airport, the woman sitting next to me and I started chatting, talking about our kids and grandkids. A few seats away was a family with four young kids who were really misbehaving. As these kids were bopping and jiving around us, the woman asked me, "Do you remember the time when you really just wanted to pick your kids up and throw them out the window?"

Whenever an aversion to what's happening arises, we acknowledge it and notice the strength of its energy. We can touch the sensation with our kind awareness and connect with it from a place of tenderness and caring, befriending it rather than resisting it. If we can't let things into our heart, we are inhibiting the wonderful energy that flows outward from our core. Trying to get rid of our aversions without first opening through the center of them simply doesn't work. The reason is pretty straightforward—under our aversions fear is always lurking.

There are three ways to skillfully respond to the second hindrance, both during meditation and in our daily lives. We can narrow our focus, broaden our focus, or divert our focus.

During a meditation session, for example, let's say that someone is breathing very loudly. It feels intrusive, and we feel anger beginning to well up. We can narrow our focus by concentrating on our own breath or broaden it by incorporating the sound of the birds outside the window or the wind, rain, or street traffic. To divert our focus, we silently repeat a mantra, practice loving-kindness meditation, visualize a mandala, or focus on something physical, like a mala. We'll look at the aperture of focus in more detail in chapter 7, when we examine focused and unfocused meditation.

When I was first asked to give talks at our Zen center, I was petrified and angry that my teacher pushed me to do this without asking me how I felt about it. I was sure I would make a fool of myself. But as I experimented with redirecting my focus, the nervousness vanished. My desire to give a good talk became a desire to support those in attendance. The moment before I began my talk, I looked at everyone in the room while holding in my heart the question, "How can I best support them?"

And it worked!

In certain situations, narrowing our focus can be equally effective in daily life. If you're worried about some future event, try narrowing your focus to a present activity. Or if you are in a threatening situation, you can narrow your focus even more. For example, if you're ridge hiking and the edge gets too close for comfort, you can laser-focus on "one step, one breath." It's empowering to realize how much control we have on our mental energy.

HINDRANCE THREE:
LETHARGY, APATHY, AND BOREDOM

When the mind fog of the third hindrance sets in, it deprives us of our natural energy and vitality. We may have trouble even getting out of bed in the morning. Our mind feels dull, cloudy, and resists any effort toward concentration or clarity. The third hindrance can be difficult to overcome. Usually, it means that we have nothing in our lives that we aspire to; we are cut off from our deepest aspirations.

Throughout my first year of practice, I experienced a lot of lethargy and sluggishness. When I shared this with Suzuki, he gazed at me with his piercing eyes for a moment, and then said, "You can learn to be just like Bodhidharma." He pointed to a two-foot-tall doll of Bodhidharma, one of Zen's most legendary ancestors for his meditative diligence. It was weighted to pop back up whenever it was knocked over. The Japanese kids at our temple loved knocking it over and watching it pop back up. To demonstrate his point, Suzuki went over to it and knocked it over several times.

That night I dreamed that I was taking turns with a little boy, knocking Bodhidharma over and watching him pop back up. Each time it righted itself, the little boy screamed with delight. I was invigorated by this dream. My lethargy vanished. I began to meditate daily and even started signing up for retreats.

Surprisingly, friends began to comment about how disciplined I was. However, discipline has never been one of my strengths. On the contrary, I slept through class after class when I was an undergraduate at Stanford. But I was energized by my big dream and encouraged by Suzuki's support.

Committing to a goal and sticking to it focus the mind and give it direction—even if that's only committing to meditate for the next ten breaths. If ten breaths are all you can muster, then do ten breaths—but do it with microsecond attentiveness. At the end of ten breaths, you may be surprised to discover that you're ready for ten more.

And of course, some degree of mental dullness and sleepiness is inevitable if you are unwavering in your practice, especially during retreats. It's natural to space out from time to time when you are stilling your mind and sitting with no stimulation or entertainment. Then the bell rings ending the meditation, and suddenly you're very alert, energized, and ready for the next activity. It happens all the time. Over the long run, not judging the quality of our meditation is a sure recipe for success.

Sometimes dullness and boredom are about resistance. We tire of our commitment to our work, to our partner, to our meditation practice. Rather than paying attention to what we're doing, we start dreaming of being elsewhere, with someone else, at some other job, or following some other spiritual practice. Perhaps we unconsciously cultivate our dullness to avoid tough decisions. Our conditioned mind is crafty. It's attractive to resist unpleasant decisions; however, skillful means is not about avoiding unpleasantness—it's about opening through the center of whatever you are experiencing.

HINDRANCE FOUR: RESTLESSNESS AND WORRY

During meditation, our mind often leaps from one thing to another—next week's schedule, a conversation that went badly, or maybe the plot of an old movie playing over and over. Restlessness is the opposite of the third hindrance where the mind feels like a big blob of dullness. When we're restless, our mind bounces around like a ping-pong ball. We may feel jumpy, irritated, and edgy.

The practice is to open through the center of restlessness, to watch where the ping-pong ball bounces from and what it bounces to. What stories are we telling ourselves? Often there's a specific emotion underlying our restlessness that's invariably tied to sensations within our body. Just transferring our attention to our sensations may be all it takes to dissolve restlessness.

If, for example, you keep thinking about your relationship with a partner or spouse, you can move your attention away from your relationship problems and investigate where sensations are showing up in the body. Then, move into the underlying worry that's showing up. Maybe you're worried about being alone.

Worry is a key aspect of restlessness—worries about imagined futures, possible failures, and damage to our self-image all contribute to feelings of restlessness. We may feel threatened by shame, guilt, or regret. Trying to put worry aside doesn't work. Again, opening through the center of our worry, observing what triggered it, experiencing the physical sensation, and watching it move through the body will give us relief.

Chronic worry, on the other hand, can be a different can of worms. It can signal agitated depression or an anxiety disorder and may require professional support. But in many cases, worry can be managed through meditation, exercise, getting enough sleep, and being honest and ethical in our actions and our interactions.

Regardless of how worry or restlessness shows up, it's important to let our meditation be what it is. Judging the quality of our meditation when our mind is restless can make us feel like frauds. Let restlessness or worry come in. Notice when restlessness and worry are not present; be grateful for those moments, take them into your heart, and allow them to nourish your practice.

HINDRANCE FIVE: DEBILITATING DOUBT

We have no reason to distrust our world, for it is not against us. If our world has fears, they are our fears. If it has an abyss, it belongs to us. If dangers appear, we must try to love them. And if we will live with faith in the value of what is challenging, then what seems most difficult will become our truest and most trustworthy friend. . . . Perhaps every terror is, at its core, something helpless that wants our help.

—Rainer Maria Rilke

The fifth hindrance can be difficult to penetrate and overcome. It can so confound the mind as to stop our practice cold. Debilitating doubt often manifests as the voice in our head that tells us we are not enough. Left unchecked, this voice can become all-consuming and so seductive that we may not even realize we're being lured into a deep pit of inertia or hopelessness.

When we notice these heavy feelings, the path forward begins when we hush the inner tyrant. The best place to do this is in meditation, where we're so attentive to our thoughts that they can't slip up on us unnoticed. We notice the first thought, let it go without comment or criticism, and return our awareness to our breath or some other object of meditation. We may not be able to stop the first thought, but we can stop the second if we're paying close enough attention.

Eventually, as the mental noise quiets down, we may find ourselves in direct contact with the heavy feelings that the noise has allowed us to avoid. Treating these feelings with compassion and kindness can break up the seemingly impenetrable mass of negativity and confusion. Whatever its root cause, it's important to remember that debilitating doubt is learned, and so can be unlearned with tender attentiveness.

We may identify the root cause of doubt by noticing when we are being indecisive or when we're holding back, whether it's in our meditation practice or some other aspect of our lives. We can develop the habit of focusing on our breath and then broadening our focus to our immediate emotional state and the accompanying sensations. Keep returning, over and over, until some clarity arises. Then, be decisive. Make a commitment to an appropriate action and stick to it.

Doubts around our meditation practice can be very specific. They could target the teacher, the teachings, or our ability to do the practice. It's very common for people to experience some level of doubt when anticipating a meditation retreat—sometimes just for a few minutes after the retreat begins and sometimes lasting throughout the entire retreat. It is good to remember that retreats are meant to be difficult. They are designed to be an ordeal, to trigger whatever you're trying to avoid, which is the first step in freeing yourself from it.

Doubt, in and of itself, is not a problem when we learn how to deal with it. It becomes a problem when we view it as confirmation of previous misgivings. This may create a self-fulfilling prophecy.

If your confidence begins to dwindle, the problem may be that you're clinging to some grand goal of enlightenment or the belief that you'll be able to calm your mind once and for all. Once you've recognized the root cause of your doubt, simply shift your attention to your body and take a few deep, mindful breaths.

Debilitating doubt can arise at any time, whether you are new to meditation or a seasoned practitioner, so it's best to learn how to navigate it skillfully as soon as possible. Often, it goes hand in hand with feeling plagued by unresolved emotional, career, or lifestyle questions.

Once again, please note that addressing the fifth hindrance is not a rejection of all doubt. Sometimes, the doubt we're experiencing is of a different nature. Cautionary doubt, as opposed to debilitating doubt, beckons us to slow down, be careful, perhaps even reconsider some decision we've made. Learning to distinguish between the two types of doubt is vital.

Doubt is sometimes a call for careful consideration. The doubt we are experiencing may be spot-on, cautioning us to proceed carefully. In daily life, our doubting mind may caution us against making a choice before we have thoroughly examined alternatives.

In the early years of my practice, after meeting Suzuki Roshi and Master Hsuan Hua and moving through the honeymoon phase with each of them, I tried the Vedanta Society for a while.

I was desperate to sink deeply into my psyche, as others I'd read about had done. I wanted to discover that great well of timelessness and the water of contentment that lies at its center.

But I couldn't make up my mind. This process of careful deliberation, prompted by cautionary doubt, went on for months. And in the end, I was able to choose a practice that has resonated with me for more than fifty years—and counting.

In spiritual practice, there is yet another kind of doubt that I would be remiss not to mention here: great doubt.

Great Doubt: Deep Questioning as a Practice

Great doubt is a double-edged sword capable of cutting through layers of built-up residue and sediment, allowing us to tap into a wellspring of innate aliveness and love of life. At the same time, it cuts through complacency and loosens our dependency on preconceived ideas.

Unlike many spiritual practices, Zen practitioners do not lean on a god or other authority figure. What Zen master Hakuin called great doubt is just as important as trust in our practice. Doubt is our ally, helping us weigh our choices and investigate conventional truisms.

It can be so easy to fall into "doubt denial" with a spiritual practice because we don't want to pay the price of giving up our attachment to "received wisdom," whether it's from a teacher, religious institution, or belief system. But skeptical doubt in spiritual and psychological exploration—as in science—is healthy and useful. In the quest to tap into a great spaciousness and clarity, both faith and doubt are equally important.

During my childhood I was exposed to two often opposing belief systems: my grandparents' Catholicism, where faith is crucial and doubt suspect, and my parents Unitarianism, where doubt is crucial and faith suspect. While my grandparents encouraged me to pray, my parents encouraged me to question all so-called religious beliefs or doctrines.

Then, just before I turned twenty-one, I was introduced to Zen meditation, where faith and doubt are equally important. Or one could say that it's important that we have enough faith to stay with the process of deeply doubting—which includes doubting the nature of the self as a separate, independent entity. Through skeptical doubt and faith in the practice, I was able to move into deeper and deeper levels of being.

Great doubt challenges us to question and investigate. It challenges us to ask the big questions. When you find yourself stuck in a specific emotion, you might ask, "*Who* is this self that is stuck? *Who* is upset? *Who* is angry? *Who* is depressed? *Who* is nervous? *Who* is struggling? *Who* wants to be enlightened? *Who* is asking the question?"

If you keep asking *who? who? who?* you may reach a point where the questioner dissolves, leaving only a feeling of joyful intimacy and profound love. Now you are experiencing the core of your being, which is the core of *all* being.

"Be a lamp unto yourself," was the Buddha's final teaching. As his disciples crowded around him and pleaded for wisdom, this was his dying wish for all those who follow him.

And it is my living wish for you.

5

UNHOOKING THE SMALL
SELF FROM ENLIGHTENMENT

Maybe you're searching in the branches
for what only appears in the roots.

—Rumi

Spiritual practice begins when we stop searching through the
leaves and branches and start digging around in the roots. Even
after the leaves and branches no longer grab our attention, we
have to dig through a lot of encrusted dirt to begin to appreciate
the depth of the roots.

Gradually, as our meditation ripens and the conditioned
patterns and emotional reactivity that have encrusted our heart
fall away, the potential arises for true happiness, freedom, and
well-being. Even if our heart opens for only a moment, that's
okay—that's all it takes.

It only takes a moment because we live in an interconnected
universe. Each moment is the eternal *NOW* that thoroughly penetrates past, present, and future. That means when the heart
opens, even for a single moment, right there lies the potential
for lasting change.

When we fully marry ourselves to this moment, and this moment, and this moment—we develop the ability to live with ease and grace. It happens naturally as we unhook our small, conditioned self from our ideas about enlightenment and simply allow the process to unfold on its own. This is the promise of spiritual practice—and the journey begins by exposing the storyteller.

EXPOSING THE STORYTELLER

We are a changing process, not a fixed being.
There never was a self—only our identification makes us think so.

—Jack Kornfield

Our identification with the storyteller convinces us that we are isolated beings. According to early Buddhist psychology, our identity—our sense of a separate, independent self—is actually the coalescing of five elements of experience which are woven together.

What we refer to as the "self" is merely a fabrication made up of five sequential processes, the fifth of which congeals into a narrator who tends to dominate the first four in an unhealthy manner. Deep-seeing vidya, the practice introduced in chapter 3, is about cultivating the ability to witness this process *as it plays out*. It's easy to go back and connect the dots in hindsight—not so easy to witness the process in the moment.

By exposing the moment-by-moment birth and dominance of the narrator/storyteller, we remove the confusion about why we do what we do. Only then do we have the ability to make choices that lead to happiness and well-being.

So let's look at each of these five elements of experience—often referred to in traditional Buddhism as the five aggregates—

and see how the fifth one takes over to shape your beliefs about yourself and your world. Listed here, in the sequence in which they arise, are the five elements that constitute our human experience:

1. Form: an interaction with the physical world
2. Sensation/feeling
3. Perception/labeling
4. Impulse
5. Consciousness: narration/storytelling

It's important to recognize that this discussion greatly oversimplifies reality as it actually unfolds. In actuality, within each moment there exists a multitude of interactions with the physical world and a waterfall of conscious and unconscious experiences. For the sake of this discussion, however, we'll take a single event and follow it through.

Form: The first aggregate, form, refers to a specific isolated event. For example, as I'm writing this, I glanced up and noticed a small red shape perched on a limb in the tree outside my window.

Sensation/feeling: Here we are not referring to "our feelings" or an emotional state such as anger, sadness, fear, anxiety, or any of the more complex emotions. This second aggregate is the most basic layer of experience; it happens even before it can be registered by our conscious awareness. Think of it as an impression existing in only three possible states: pleasant, unpleasant, and neutral. Neutral simply means the impression is not strong enough to evoke a pleasant or unpleasant response in us. When I see the red shape in tree, I get a pleasant feeling.

Perception/labeling: The third aggregate arises the moment you realize something has happened, recognize it having an impact on your world, and give it a label. I may label the red shape perched on a limb outside my window as a cardinal. Or if I don't know what kind of bird it is, I may just label it a red bird.

Impulse: The fourth aggregate is where you begin to form a judgment about the event that was registered and labeled in the third aggregate. The judgment you form—which happens instantaneously—determines the impulse. Both judgment and impulse depend on past conditioning. Your past conditioning has a direct effect on the way you perceive and interpret future experiences. In the case of the cardinal in the tree, my impulse is to call out to my wife, telling her there's a cardinal in the tree—because in a Minnesota winter, there's so little color that a red bird can light up the whole yard, and I don't want her to miss it.

Consciousness: The fifth aggregate, consciousness, our storytelling capacity, is wonderful. But too often, the storyteller dominates the first four aggregates to the extent that we don't even notice them. This storytelling ability may be unique to human beings, and it is the glue that holds cultures together. And every story needs a storyteller, even a made-up one.

However, it is this fabricated storyteller that causes us the most problems. We are so caught by it and the narratives it weaves that we lose our connection with the first four aggregates, which are the ones that keep us grounded in reality. It's quite apparent how the storyteller can easily create all sorts of real-world problems. For example, if I'm in a rotten mood and I notice someone yawning during one of my dharma talks, I may blame the person yawning: *This guy just doesn't get it.* Or, if I'm feeling self-conscious that day, I may weave a story about how terrible I am at connecting with people.

On the other hand, if the story I weave is one of gratitude and appreciation, as in the red cardinal outside my window and the warm feeling I get from seeing it, the effects can be quite wonderful.

The storyteller can and will weave endless scenarios forever. For as long as we reflect endlessly on the scenarios playing out in our mind, the fifth aggregate dominates our life. As the narrative grows and expands, increasing its hold on us, it will influence everything we do.

When the storyteller takes over, chattering on and on, we lose our connection to the present. The first four aggregates are present-moment experiences—they ground us in the here and now—and present-moment experiences happen very rapidly. But the storyteller can entrance us endlessly, spinning yarn after yarn.

My wife and I may get into a delightful conversation about how to attract more cardinals into our yard in winter. We may talk about how lucky we are to have one that comes regularly, bringing a little joy into the bare Minnesota landscape at this time of year. As long as we don't get so caught up in the story about cardinals that we forget to notice and appreciate the swarms of sparrows alighting in the tree right now, there's no problem.

Early Buddhist psychology assures us it's possible to free ourselves from the storyteller's domination by bringing the aggregates into view—a practice that meditators have relied on for hundreds of years. As we devote our awareness to the aggregates that keep us grounded in the present, we are depriving the storyteller the mental space and energy it requires to dominate and override our immediate experience.

Bringing the aggregates into view allows us to distinguish between our moment-to-moment experiences (the first, second, third, and fourth layers of experience) and the ideas and stories we fabricate (the fifth layer). Only when we're able to witness the making of the story as it unfolds do we have the freedom to choose differently.

THE TYRANNY OF A SINGLE DESCRIPTION

A human being has so many skins inside, covering the depths of the heart. We know so many things, but we don't know ourselves! Why, thirty or forty skins or hides, as thick and hard as an ox's or bear's, cover the soul. Go into your own ground and learn to know yourself there.

—Meister Eckhart

The practice of vidya is exactly the kind of deep seeing that allows us to penetrate our hardened beliefs, habits, and emotions—*thirty or forty skins or hides, as thick and hard as an ox's or bear's*—that cover the depths of our heart.

Bare awareness meditation, which we'll be talking about throughout this book, is the key to developing vidya. It's also the foundation of Zen practice. It means paying nonjudgmental attention to each skin—each layer of thought, each feeling, and each emotion. As we thoroughly penetrate each skin, we sink down into our own ground and get to know ourselves there. The sinking down part happens on its own; it is Suzuki's fortunate accident.

Bare awareness glues us to the present so we are not so consumed by either our regrets or our projections. Only then can we marry ourselves, moment by moment, to each activity. When I mentioned this in one of my dharma talks, somebody said, "But aren't before and after important?"

"Of course," I replied, "they're vitally important." The key is to learn how to relate to the past and future without being consumed by them. When it's time to plan, we plan. When it's time to execute, we let go of the planning and execute. Even if things fall apart, we stay in the present. We bring to bear the newly discovered insights that failure provides, create a new plan, and then we execute it.

A committed meditation practice allows us to sink into our own ground and know ourselves there. Over and over, we lay bare our own heart and allow the depths of our own aliveness to spring forth. Zen master Linji, the founder of Rinzai Zen, called this "letting the person of naked red flesh come forth."

Years ago, I sat in meditation every morning at the Zen center in San Francisco, which was on a very busy one-way street with traffic rushing toward downtown. I found its cacophony distracting, and even distressing, as I tried to stay focused on my breath.

Then I happened to read something by the avant-garde musician John Cage. He talked about attending a series of talks by D. T. Suzuki (no relation to Shunryu Suzuki) at Columbia University.

Cage spoke of D. T. Suzuki's soft voice that was frequently drowned out by the roar of planes from a nearby airport. Cage became increasingly frustrated, until, at some point, he experienced a shift. He began to notice how Suzuki's soft voice and the roar overhead had a way of complementing each other. Frustration gave way to curiosity. Cage talked about how this experience informed the way he created music for the rest of his career.

After I read how Cage welcomed dissonant sounds into his music, I began to welcome the traffic noise into the meditation hall. That's when I realized that a calm mind is not a fragile mind. That was just my idea—one that, once recognized, I happily let go.

John Cage was able to dissolve the hard skin of frustration that caused his heart to contract against what was happening. When his heart reopened, he uncovered the fruits of the present moment. This is what Zen meditation does for us. Through practice, we cultivate the ability to welcome each thought, each feeling, each note, as a melody that becomes a wonderful song: the song of life, or even better, the song of life/death—the song that includes everything.

BREAKING THROUGH YOUR MASTER NARRATIVE

Meditation practice is about opening up to your big, interconnected Self. This is not the small, frightened ego-self that always needs to be protected and defended—that's just your conditioned mind stealing the show.

Self-realization, however, is not easy. At times, you'll feel the pull to fall back into the comfort of your conditioned views and beliefs. But as our awareness expands through this practice, so does our ability to live from a much deeper place.

In addition to the narratives our storyteller weaves, each of us was born into an overarching master narrative. If you were born into extreme poverty, for instance—as many people are even in the United States—the master narrative may convince you that economic independence, travel, adventure, and even a college education are beyond your reach.

At the other end of the spectrum are those born into wealth and power. The master narrative from which their life unfolds includes all the tools and support they need to take their place among those who are well-educated and prosperous. They are destined to move into powerful positions, and anything less is inconceivable.

Moving beyond your master narrative, regardless of what it

is, is the beginning of spiritual maturity. Even for the rich and powerful, deviating from the beliefs and values of your family often leads to rejection by those whose approval you most earnestly crave. It can be mentally confusing and emotionally disorienting.

I was born into a prestigious family and grew up in Palo Alto, California. I went to Stanford University, as my father, mother, and grandfather did. The master narrative demanded that I would become a doctor or a lawyer. When my father despaired that I would do neither, he suggested hopefully, "Perhaps he can at the least become a dentist." To both my father and grandfather, who was a justice on the California Supreme Court, anything less was unacceptable—an embarrassment.

But a strange thing happened just before I turned twenty-one years old. I met a Japanese man who had only been in this country for a few years. Suzuki Roshi turned my life upside down. Soon after meeting him, I totally abandoned the master narrative forged by my family history. Stepping off that path was both confusing and uncertain, but I was buoyed by a lightness that seemed to emanate from Suzuki.

More and more, I came to believe that I could move beyond the master narrative that I'd been clothed in since birth. I could experience for myself the joyfulness and freedom that my teacher seemed to exude.

The spiritual path is one of perpetual becoming, but not becoming someone or something through birth and conditioning. On the contrary, it is one of continually shedding those old, conditioned ideas passed down from generation to generation. Only then can we experience the present moment, free of our master narrative which becomes a mere remnant of the past, and free of the imposed expectations to carry that remnant into the future, imposing it on the next generation.

Do not dwell in the past;
Do not dream of the future.
Concentrate the mind on this moment.

—The Buddha

SKINWALKING AND TAKING
THE EXQUISITE RISK

Each of us has thought and behavior patterns—our stories about ourselves—that reify our sense of self, holding it firmly in place in our psyche. Imagining these conditioned patterns as old, dried-up skins creates a felt sense of being confined by them, constrained by their extra weight. When you allow yourself to fully experience this constriction, the desire arises to shed that extra weight so you can move gracefully and fluidly through life.

In Buddhism, the iconic skin-shedder is the great serpent, or serpent-dragon. The serpent is also a visual embodiment of fluidity, grace, and flow. A serpent moves like a wave through water. In Buddhist mythology, the great serpent is also the protector and purveyor of wisdom.

The Sanskrit word for great serpent is *naga*. The traditional Buddhist naga is a deity that takes the form of a giant cobra, often with multiple heads. And a serpent king, called Mucalinda, plays an important role in the Buddhist creation myth. Mucalinda, with his three heads, emerged from beneath the earth to protect the Buddha as he sat under the bodhi tree. The Buddha sat in meditation for seven days in his final quest for enlightenment, shedding layer after layer of limited beliefs. He did this by allowing these beliefs to arise in his consciousness without fear or judgment, studying each belief closely, and then watching as it dissolved.

In this creation myth heralding the birth of Buddhism, the serpent king Mucalinda symbolizes the wholeness of reality. Mucalinda emerged from beneath the earth, from the ground of all being, to purvey the wisdom of transformation upon the Buddha. After his enlightenment, the Buddha, which is a title meaning "awakened one," no longer experienced himself as an isolated being separate from the fabric of the universe.

As meditators, we can call on our serpent power to help us shed layers upon layers of gunk we've carried for way too long. With each skin we shed, we experience more lightness and freedom because each new skin is more porous, more sensitive, and more permeable than the previous one.

Poet and author Mark Nepo talks about taking "the exquisite risk."[7] Each time we shed a skin, even though we're taking a risk, we feel more alive. And it's not just the shedding of painful memories or beliefs; we also shed those memories and beliefs that have given us comfort and a sense of security, exposing ourselves to some perceived danger and loss. But spiritual practice is about living fully by letting go of the comforting and the familiar. This path of exquisite risk arises in each moment that we are willing to be fully present and fully alive.

An interesting variation of the practice of skin shedding is *skinwalking,* which is a concept of Indigenous peoples around the world. Take the Diné (Navajo), for example. A traditional Diné belief holds that shamans can take the form of bears, wolves, and eagles for the purpose of healing and protecting their communities. Skinwalking, like skin shedding, is about releasing our sense of a separate and bounded self.

When I lived at the Tassajara Zen Monastery, Suzuki Roshi gave a talk every night. Back then we had no electricity in the meditation hall. Under the soft glow of a lantern, his face often seemed to undulate—sometimes a man was teaching us; other times his face appeared to be distinctly feminine. The original gender-switcher in Buddhist mythology sometimes manifests as Avalokiteshvara, a young male, and other times as Kuan Yin or

Kannon, both females. Whatever the gender, their appearance represents the arising in our consciousness of a deep feeling of interbeing.

Fear causes us to shrink up and cling to our hardened skin. Perhaps the most dominant component of fear is rigidity, and closely associated to rigidity is aggression. We see it every day in American culture—including in our ideas about gender. How interesting it is to see a younger generation of people who are exploring gender with a greater sense of fluidity and lightness, including transcending the gender binary altogether.

Our ego-self is organized around fear. It has a strong need to control, to hold tight to whatever offers a sense of security and comfort and contract against anything that makes us feel vulnerable. But we have the potential to let go of our habitual projections and protections, despite our instinctual dependence on them.

Watching the moon
at dawn,
solitary, mid-sky,
I knew myself completely:
no part left out.
—Enlightenment poem by Izumi Shikibu[8]

6

HERE AND NOW

Staying Present with Mantras, Malas, and Gathas

Mantras, malas, and gathas are meditative tools that help us open up to deeper states of consciousness. During my first three or four years with Suzuki Roshi, he refused to discuss meditative tools or techniques of any kind. "Just sit," he would say. But over the years, he began to soften up. Today, when I work with students, we explore all the tools in our toolbox because a committed meditation practice can be very difficult.

Regardless of which tool we are working with, however, it is important to remember that we cannot call forth our calm mind and peaceful heart through willpower. We can't force it, no matter how hard we try. It happens on its own, in its own time, and in its own way. And when it does, it feels like an experience that you fall into—a serendipitous *accident*. The moment you try to control, define, deepen, or extend it, you are returned, unceremoniously, to your small, chattering mind.

About twenty years ago, I visited Bhutan, which is known for its temples and monasteries. As we drove and walked through the countryside, I saw OM MANI PADME HUM etched into rock outcroppings everywhere. Later, I spent about three days at a monastery that was only accessible by trail, where I was joined by a group of monks working with their malas or prayer beads. As they worked, they were reciting OM MANI PADME HUM, over and over. That's where I discovered its meaning: jewel in the lotus. The lotus is honored in Buddhist teaching because it grows in muddy water.

As I write this, our country—and particularly Minneapolis—is immersed in the muddy water of both the global pandemic and the social turmoil arising after the murder of George Floyd by a police officer. Right here in the muddy water of my own neighborhood is where I have an opportunity to turn all this cultural friction into a lotus flower. And to do that, sometimes we might need one of the meditative tools to help us make that transformation.

MANTRAS: A MATTER OF RESONANCE

Mantra is a sound vibration through which we mindfully focus our thoughts, our feelings, and our highest intention.

—Girish

A mantra is a syllable, word, or group of words that has psychological or spiritual power. The earliest mantras go back three thousand years, when they were first used on the Indian subcontinent. The resonance that arises between a sound vibration and our thoughts, feelings, and intentions happens naturally, much like two tuning forks resonating at the same frequency. Today, there are a multitude of phrases readily available throughout the world's meditative traditions.

The word *mantra* is derived from two Sanskrit words—*manas*, meaning "mind," and *tra*, meaning "protect." Together they translate to "protection," and in some cases, "compassion." Our original, still mind is always here, but our worries and fears leak all over everything, so our original self goes unnoticed.

A mantra has the power to protect us from this leaking. And since compassion can be described as wisdom actualized, a mantra also cultivates clarity and wisdom. A mantra, then, is a tool that protects the mind, cultivates clarity and wisdom, and actualizes compassion.

Although most prominent in Eastern traditions, mantras are also used in other traditions and religions. A popular mantra for Protestant Christians is simply the name Jesus. Catholics commonly repeat the Hail Mary prayer or Ave Maria—my Catholic grandmother used to work her prayer beads continually with the Hail Mary or Ave Maria. Many Jewish practitioners recite *Baruch atah Adonai*, meaning "Blessed art thou, oh Lord."

The very first phrase I used to mindfully focus my thoughts, feelings, and highest intention—knowing almost nothing about Buddhism—was from *The Teachings of the Mystics* by W. T. Stace. It was Jesus's simple phrase, "the peace that passeth understanding." I repeated it, over and over, during a train ride from San Francisco to Salt Lake City. This was before I began a meditation practice or even knew what meditation was. I discovered that if I repeated it continually with heartfelt effort throughout the trip, I became surrounded and permeated by a feeling of deep spaciousness and joy. Once I fell into the groove of it, the sense of spaciousness sustained itself through the remainder of the trip.

Most of the mantras I have used since then are from the Buddhist tradition, with one exception. During the three or four years I spent with a Lakota spiritual guide, I followed his advice to repeat MITAKUYE OYASIN, which translates to "all my relatives." Whenever I felt walled off, as if I were somehow excluded from the interbeing nature of all life, I would chant MITAKUYE OYASIN.

MITAKUYE OYASIN reflects the Lakota worldview that all beings are interconnected. And time after time, I fell into the same deep spaciousness and joyful sense of interbeing I'd experienced many years before when I first heard it. If you do this yourself, you may find that the joyful stillness you aspire to is closer than you think, closer than even your own breath.

Teacher and author Sally Kempton said that a mantra is "a bit like rubbing a flint against a stone to strike fire."[9] She goes on to say that it's the friction between the syllables of the mantra that ignites the fire and, over time, shifts your inner state.

One way that the fire shifts your inner state is by burning through the turmoil and the incessant mental chatter that can get so stirred up during our meditation. As we come back to our word or phrase again and again, there is the potential to open into a great spaciousness that includes everything and is, at the same time, infused with a deep calm—even in the midst of so much seemingly insurmountable turmoil.

Yogis have used mantras for hundreds of years to experience the profound sense of calm that mantra practice can bring about, and Western science is finally catching up. Modern brain-imaging techniques have confirmed the benefits of this ancient practice. In one study in 2017, researchers from Linköping University in Sweden measured activity in a region of the brain called the default mode network—the area that's active when we are remembering, regretting, and rehearsing—to measure the effects of mantra practice. The researchers concluded that mantra practice induced a state of deep relaxation, and furthermore, they found that a regular practice could promote the ability to deal with life's stresses more skillfully.[10]

Mantra Practice

Find a mantra that resonates with you and try to set aside ten to twenty minutes a day to practice. Once you've chosen a specific mantra, it's best to stay with it for some months, giving it a chance to do its work, before considering a switch to another one.

Begin by sitting in a comfortable position. Repeat the mantra a few times silently, on each inhale and exhale. Don't try to focus on the mantra too hard; simply allow your body and mind to relax into it. Just like you would in any other type of meditation, when thoughts or feelings enter your mind, simply notice them and then return to silently reciting the word or phrase.

The most frequently recited mantra in the Zen tradition comes from the Heart Sutra: GATE GATE PARAGATE PARASAMGATE (*gate* is pronounced *ga-tay*). It translates to "gone, gone, gone beyond, gone completely beyond." You can repeat one word or the entire series of words.

When I was having an especially difficult time staying focused during a seven-day retreat, Suzuki Roshi suggested that I make this mantra the focus of my meditation. It was a surprising suggestion because, at that time, Suzuki had never talked about using techniques of any kind, much less mantras. All these years later, I continue to be grateful for this instruction, and I still use it whenever I'm experiencing some difficulty in my meditation.

GATE GATE PARAGATE PARASAMGATE is about going beyond our limiting beliefs, which cloud our ability to see clearly. And going beyond strongly held beliefs requires that we go beyond the three types of poisonous glue that hold these beliefs in place. The first type is greed: we grasp at any shiny object that promises immediate pleasure. The second poisonous glue is hatred: we push away anything that interferes with our getting what we want. And the third is ignorance: our tendency to ignore everything else.

So far, I have mentioned several mantras from which you may choose. Here are three more that you might find to be useful:

MAY I MEET THIS MOMENT FULLY.
MAY I MEET IT AS A FRIEND.

In the first sentence you are affirming that an alert and balanced mind, which is not caught by before or after, is a possibility for you. In the second sentence, you are affirming your ability to welcome whatever comes with an open heart.

Real, but not true

This mantra affirms that your thoughts and emotions are real—but not necessarily true. When we believe something to be true, we naturally contract around it. If you can relax into this short but insightful mantra, new meanings and possibilities may be revealed.

Things as it is

This expression originated with Suzuki Roshi and has since become a popular mantra. While grammatically incorrect—which I foolishly pointed out to him once—Suzuki's odd nomenclature has a unifying effect. It acknowledges conventional reality, which is often referred to in Buddhism as "the 10,000 things"—and then, in the same breath, affirms the no-thingness of ultimate reality.

Choosing a mantra is not complicated. Just select one that resonates with you, engages you, and burns through your mental chatter. Thich Nhat Hanh suggested "DEEP" on the in-breath and "PEACE" on the out-breath, or "PRESENT MOMENT" on the in-breath and "ONLY MOMENT" on the out-breath. It really can be that simple—and at the same time quite powerful.

The nineteenth-century poet Alfred Lord Tennyson discovered that he could calm his mind by merely sitting still and repeating his own name. Here's how he described the experience: "My individuality itself seems to dissolve and fade away into boundless being . . . the loss of personality seeming no extinction, but the one true life."[11]

I'm sure it's obvious by now that the specific mantra is not so important. What is important is consistency and engagement. When you catch yourself trying to empower the mantra yourself, just return to the actual practice of pouring your whole body and mind into the mantra and letting go of any thought of gain or loss. Your effort is to simply be present with the mantra—wherever it takes you, there you are, fully present and at one with the mantra, which, within itself, includes all beings.

MALAS: ENGAGING YOUR SENSE OF TOUCH

A traditional Buddhist mala consists of 108 beads, one mountain bead, and a tassel. The number one symbolizes the universe or reality, zero symbolizes emptiness, and the eight is for infinity or timelessness. The mountain bead, which is larger than the others, provides a starting and ending point. The most common way to use a mala is during meditation for breath control and for reciting a mantra.

As any meditator knows, staying mindful and in the present moment while meditating isn't easy. Mala beads help to keep you in the present moment and alert as you move your fingers across the beads with each breath or each recitation of a mantra.

Mala Practice

Begin with the mala in your dominant hand, draped between the middle and index fingers. Starting at the mountain bead, use your thumb to travel around the mala, reciting your mantra, or taking a full inhale/exhale with each bead until you return to the mountain bead.

If you're using a mantra, you may whisper it, speak it aloud, or recite it in your mind, whichever feels right to you. Whichever option you choose, stick with it throughout the meditation session. If you want to do another round, just move your fingers in the opposite direction until you return to the mountain bead.

GATHAS: WORDPLAY AND AMBIGUITY

By reciting the short verses known as gathas, we transform any activity into an opportunity to awaken to our true nature.

—Zachiah Murray

Gathas are much like mantras, except that they are generally designed to help us focus on specific activities. *Gatha* is a derivative of the Sanskrit word *gai*, which loosely means "songs or verses that call us to the present moment."

According to author and teacher Zachiah Murray, gathas originated around 1300 B.C.E. through the texts of the Iranian poet and prophet Zoroaster. As Buddhism spread eastward from India, it was influenced by the Zoroastrian traditions, and today the recitation of gathas has been popularized by Zen teachers Thich Nhat Hanh and Robert Aitken. "Rich with wordplay and intentional ambiguities, these gathas are intended to awaken the innate inner wisdom of the practitioner, spurring her toward enlightenment," wrote Murray in an article published in *Lion's Roar Magazine*.[12]

Gatha Practice

At our Zen center in Minneapolis, we have gathas posted in key places for activities like waking up in the morning, brushing our teeth, taking out the garbage, or entering the meditation hall—we even have one posted by the mirror in the bathroom for shaving.

Some practitioners write gathas on sticky notes and put them on the refrigerator or the coffeepot. Others write gathas in their calendar, one for each day. Here are a few gathas that you may find useful. The first three are by Andrew Weiss, a student at our Zen center; the fourth is by Thich Nhat Hanh.

DRIVING A CAR

This car is my legs.
It goes where I choose.
When I drive with awareness,
Everyone lives in safety.

TURNING ON THE TELEVISION

Mind and television.
Receive what I choose.
I select well-being
And nourish joy.

PREPARING FOOD

Earth, water, sun, and air,
All live in this food I prepare.

BEFORE TAKING FOOD

My bowl, empty now,
will soon be filled with precious food.
Beings all over the world are struggling to live.
How fortunate we are to have this meal.

Anyone can compose their own gathas, drawing on daily experiences. It's good to choose an activity that we regularly perform. Once we've composed it, we simply memorize the gatha and then recite it each time we engage in the activity. When we do this persistently, our activities may become meditations in motion.

There are three simple steps to gatha practice: *recite, synchronize,* and *simplify.* Once the gatha is created, stay with it for as long as you're engaged in the activity. As an example, here's one that I wrote to use during my daily walk to the lake near my house.

Looking at Bde Maka Ska,
Seeing my true nature in its reflection,
Heartmind at peace.

Step one: recite. Bde Maka Ska is a lake near my house. As I approach it, I stop and take a moment to bring my awareness into each in-breath and each out-breath. I observe the beauty of the lake's shimmering surface. Then I recite the gatha.

Step two: synchronize the gatha with your breath. "Looking at Bde Maka Ska," as I breathe in; "Seeing my true nature," as I breathe out; "in its reflection," as I breathe in; "Heartmind at peace," as I breathe out.

Step three: simplify. I shorten the gatha after I have practiced with it and internalized it. Breathing in, I say, "looking." Breathing out, I say, "seeing my true nature." Breathing in and out, I say "Peace."

Here are a couple of examples of ways people use a gatha as an intervention.

If you find yourself habitually checking the weather on your phone, turn it into a meditation practice. As you click the icon, breathe in as you notice the temperature reading. Regardless of how hot or cold it is, exhale and silently say, "This is." This may help you short-circuit all the junk you usually say to yourself: *Yuck, it's going to snow! Not rain again! When is it ever going to get warm? What am I doing living here?* Instead, use the gatha to help you embrace the weather just as it is, which can bring you great peace of mind.

Social media's relentless pull offers many opportunities for gatha practice. Recently, I've been supporting someone who developed a habit during this ongoing COVID-19 pandemic of relying on TikTok as her link to the outside world. She is so caught by this habit that she incessantly asks herself, *How many likes and follows have I gotten? For which posts?* I encouraged her to cultivate the following practice.

Each time she clicks into her TikTok account, she turns her awareness inward and notices her thoughts in that moment. Breathing in, she says, "watching my thoughts." And then as she breathes out and releases them, she says, "returning to my body." The last time I met with her she was quite relieved and amazed at how well the practice worked.

I encourage you to come up with your own words or phrases to help cut through your chatter, both during meditation and in activities of everyday life. Any actions that have become mindless and automatic could use mantra or gatha support. Rote activities can become little gateways into a deep sense of calm.

Anything—literally *anything*—can be the seed for spiritual transformation.

Whichever tool you choose, if you are diligent and committed and pour your whole body and mind into each recitation or each breath, you are stumbling toward enlightenment, moment by moment—until, when you least expect it, your tangled thoughts loosen, the distinction between heart and mind falls away, and your mind becomes still.

7

THE SPIRIT AND PRACTICE OF ZEN MEDITATION

To taste the flavor of zazen [Zen meditation] you have to dip the tea bag into the hot water, again and again.

—Suzuki Roshi

When we begin a meditation practice, the first obstacle we face is often our own thoughts—they come so fast they seem to trip over each other. If we do get a moment of quiet, it's fleeting—then we're back, immersed in the chatter of a busy mind, wondering if it's even worth our effort. This is not only experienced by beginning meditators; we all feel this way from time to time.

Eventually, though, something begins to happen. Our thoughts become less substantial, more transparent. Encouraged, we double our commitment to bring deep-seeing vidya into our meditation. That's when we begin to see through the thoughts and into the patterns from which they arise.

Vidya begins with an elusive and indistinct sense that something important is happening, but the significance is just out of reach—like vague shapes just beyond the horizon of our awareness. It takes time for our inner eyes to adjust to the sensation-based language of our inner teacher.

As the elusive and indistinct something begins to clarify itself, we move into a very difficult stage of meditation practice. We become painfully aware of deep-rooted fear, anxiety, or trauma that our mental chatter was covering over, and we most likely don't want to deal with those painful emotions.

Often, people become discouraged at this point because it feels like their effort has been for nothing—even less than nothing because they feel worse than before. Instead of steeping in a profound stillness, it feels more like they're steeping in their worries, moods, regrets, confusion, and heartache. It takes courage to experience our deepest hurts in a direct and undiluted way. With a sincere meditation practice, however, there is no avoiding these feelings.

Suzuki Roshi had two expressions which, when paired together, sum up the spirit of meditation. The first one is "by washing silk many times it becomes white and soft enough to weave." If we want our meditation practice to bear fruit, we need a daily practice that we show up for, regardless of how busy or hectic our lives become.

Another obstacle that comes up again and again is getting caught by the past or the future. Our mind can get really worked up, binding us to the wheel of reacting, regretting, and rehearsing. When the wheel starts spinning, it becomes the driving force of our life, cutting us off from our interconnected nature. We feel stuck in what Zen teacher Joko Beck called "our substitute life."[13]

I hear this a lot from my students: "I can't meditate because my thoughts are too loud, too busy, too out of control." So many people are convinced that their meditative experience is worse than that of others, but the truth of this experience is its commonality—everybody feels this way.

When we cling to our ideals, we set an impossible standard for ourselves. Trying to control your mind is a dangerous stumbling block. It can lead to feelings of inadequacy and futility. Suzuki said, "If you want to control a horse, give it a large pasture." In other words, the mind does what it does, and all you can do is stay with it with kind and gentle awareness. This is the spirit of meditation.

When we step back from all our regretting and rehearsing just a little bit, we see that the world is much bigger and much warmer than we ever imagined. If we see the wheel of reactivity without judgment, there's a chance we can learn to disidentify with it. But we can't do it by *trying* to disidentify—if you're trying, then you're still caught by it. You've just moved to a different spot on the wheel.

Students often retort, "But if I don't try, how will I ever get there?" It's a fair question, a reasonable question—it's the kind of objection our small mind likes to construct. But small mind cannot understand paradox—so it cannot understand the way of Zen.

We stumble over the paradoxical nature of life again and again. A spiritual teaching of any depth will sooner or later exhaust the mind, until it finally falls silent. Again and again, we simply "dip the tea bag into the hot water."

When you're discouraged but continue to show up, it's the teacher's job to assure you that faltering is normal, even necessary. Do not try to change, deny, or ignore your feelings. Zen is about accepting reality just as it is. That includes your inner reality.

Instead of trying to get rid of your thoughts and feelings, the practice of meditation is to look at the context within which they arise. What is the emotional environment surrounding them? Is it fear? Frustration? Worry?

This meditative investigation is always to be done with an open heart and gentle awareness. In this way our churning mind becomes our teacher, revealing fixations and patterns so we can heal. This is how we cultivate vidya. This is how we stumble toward enlightenment.

FOUR STAGES OF MEDITATIVE AWARENESS

With a sustained daily meditation practice, we can typically mark four distinct stages of development. Initially, since our lives tend to be very busy, we are motivated by a sense that meditation will bring some calm and clarity into our chaotic life. Eventually, however, this first stage of practice, with its focus on a particular outcome, becomes a stumbling block.

Please don't beat yourself up when you recognize that you're doing this. Instead, move your awareness directly into the feeling that supports this need to attain something. If you stay with it long enough, you're bound to touch an underlying fear, along with the sensations connected to it. This fear is about needing to protect yourself. If it arose from some deep-seated childhood trauma, it may even be a survival fear. Or it may not be trauma-related at all but stem simply from the stresses and demands of modern life. Take Phil, for example.

Phil is a midlevel manager at a health care organization. He was obsessed with hitting his quarterly targets, so he pushed himself and his staff relentlessly. He feared being fired, or even having to quit because of his anxiety. After about a year of daily meditation and participating in retreats, he asked to meet with me. "It's been a year," he complained during our meeting, "and I still have this anxiety." He felt like he was not making any progress at all.

I asked him how things were going, both at work and in his life in general. He talked about his moods and reactivity. It became apparent that he had learned a lot about himself during his year of practice, and I pointed out that he had been quite unaware of his patterns when he began meditating.

Phil realized that, for the first time in his life, he was able to see his fear-based thinking, judgments, and beliefs without criticizing himself or his staff. Even though he was still experiencing a lot of anxiety, it no longer limited his effectiveness at work. Phil had moved into the second stage of meditative awareness, the "What can I learn about myself?" stage.

This next stage of meditative awareness is where we encounter Suzuki Roshi's second expression: "By hitting iron when it's hot, we make it strong and sharp, like a sword." This expression has quite a different feel to it than the first one: "By washing silk many times it becomes white and soft enough to weave." The "hitting iron when it's hot" stage can be quite difficult physically and mentally. Phil's mental state and emotions flared up quite frequently, and during meditation he often became agitated or "hot." I assured him that this is common. That heat he was experiencing actually helps us move beyond the small, complaining self from which our chatter arises.

So Phil hung in there. He continued to meditate daily, and we met frequently one to one. He noticed how quickly he wanted to jump in and control everything and everyone. Recognizing these impulses, he was able to resist acting them out. As he got better at managing his own anxiety-induced impulses, his stress level decreased, as did that of others in his office. He had moved into the third stage of meditative awareness, a stage I call, "What can I discover about my relationships and how can I deepen them?"

Gradually, all serious meditators become free from their addictive chatter by patiently allowing the mind to cleanse itself. As your chattering mind slows down, you become less self-absorbed, and you notice how your behavior affects others. In the noticing, your attitude and behavior toward others begin to change. It happens naturally, on its own, because heart-mind is naturally compassionate. To experience a sense of connection, we just have to remove the barriers, which are always fear-based.

Phil developed an intimate relationship with his fears and vulnerabilities. He was able to talk about them openly and honestly, without judgment or pretense, allowing a more intimate relationship with those around him. He listened to his staff more, which inspired his team. He spoke from his heart more, which deepened his personal relationships with friends and family.

As Phil moved into the final stage of meditative awareness, he began to experience moments of deep silence, not just in his mind but in his entire body. The embodiment experienced at this stage may be fleeting, but a moment of this depth is beginningless and endless, because it is not of time. This reverberating effect has the power to effect lasting change.

It is here where a sincere and committed meditation practice bears the sweetest fruit. What is experienced in these moments becomes the birthplace of the kind of calm confidence and inner strength that doesn't abandon us during difficult times.

As your need to control dissolves, fear is replaced by trust, and with it comes an abiding stillness that penetrates your skin, flesh, bone, and marrow. Living wakefully from your own still center, which is the center of all life, is now available to you, moment by moment.

TWO TYPES OF ZEN MEDITATION

Seated meditation is the fundamental practice for all schools of Zen. We meditate to let go of our preconceived ideas so we're not tossed around so much by our thoughts and beliefs.

An obstacle for many meditators is the notion that meditation is a state without thoughts. However, we are rarely free of thoughts. Meditation is not about stopping your thoughts; we don't meditate to transform into a stone. With a daily meditation practice, the thought stream becomes more like background noise—you're aware of it, but not bothered or distracted by it.

Zen meditation includes both focused and unfocused meditation. Both methods move the thought stream from the forefront of our attention to the background. As meditators, it's important to become adept at both types.

Focused Meditation

In focused meditation, we limit our field of awareness by training our attention on our breath or a mantra. Becoming adept in focused meditation is necessary so we can cut through our obsessive monkey mind and tap into the space between our thoughts.

Many years ago, I was sitting in a long retreat with Suzuki Roshi. Just outside the meditation hall was a fast-flowing creek. As we all sat facing the wall, Suzuki said, "It only takes one rock to disturb the natural flow of the creek. All you need to do in your meditation is remove that one rock."

Focused meditation is about dislodging one rock, then another, then another. There's the obsession rock, the worry rock, the regret rock, the fantasy rock. Whatever your rock may be, see it, hang out with it a while with kind, gentle attention, give it all the space it needs to air its grievance, and then release it, allowing it to return to the stream of quietude and stillness that includes everything—even the rocks.

So there's no need to stumble or falter during your meditation because of the rocks. Zen master Ryokan said:

The water of the valley stream
Never shouts at the tainted world
"Purify yourself!"[14]

Unfocused Meditation: Bare Awareness

The second type is bare awareness meditation. Instead of trying to remove the rock, we receive all the sensations and feelings within our experience, as if each were a gift from the universe.

As I mentioned earlier, the San Francisco Zen Center was on a very busy street when I practiced there, and one of the regular meditation sessions took place during rush hour. My struggle with the traffic noise waxed and waned from day to day, depending on my mood, stress level, or even how much sleep I had gotten the night before. On one particular morning, however, this struggling suddenly dropped away. I found myself enjoying the noises.

That morning, Ryokan's valley stream teaching hit home for me in a very profound way. My concerns about rocks and noise flowed unhindered with the valley stream as I sat, bathed in stillness. And for the rest of that morning, I no longer felt the urge to shout at the tainted world.

In bare awareness meditation, we pay attention to everything that is happening, giving no one object precedence over others. It is simply nonjudgmental awareness of anything and everything, inside and outside, including our senses, emotions, and thoughts.

BARE AWARENESS OF BODILY SENSATIONS

In Zen, bodily sensations are of great importance and value. Zen emphasizes the practice of getting out of your head and realizing that your own body, including all its limitations, is the very body of Buddha.

In American culture, Walt Whitman (1819–1892) was one of the earliest poets to write about the sacredness of the body, rejecting the puritanical beliefs of our founders. "I Sing the Body

Electric" shocked straitlaced New Englanders, who believed that bodily pleasure in any form was an example of our sinful and fallen state.

As a member of the transcendentalist movement, Whitman focused on the nondifferentiation between the sacred and mundane—and even profane. "I Sing the Body Electric" is too long to include here, but to give you a little taste, here's the first verse.

I sing the body electric,
The armies of those I love engirth me and I engirth them,
They will not let me off till I go with them, respond to them,
And discorrupt them, and charge them full with the charge of the soul.[15]

Whitman and his fellow New Englanders of the transcendentalist movement relished the rich experience of the body—extolling the virtues of taste, touch, sight, smell, and sound. They developed a small but impactful counterculture.

A century later, while the dominant culture was still mistrustful of sensual pleasure, a burgeoning American counterculture was blooming as a reaction against post–World War II repression. In the early 1970s, you would find *The Joy of Sex* right next to *The Heart Sutra* on my bookshelf.

Our counterculture was simpatico with Zen in many ways, including the emphasis on being fully engaged in the physically and sexually expressive side of life. German-born Gestalt psychotherapist Fritz Perls captured the mood perfectly in his oft-repeated catchphrase, "Lose your mind and come to your senses."

This integration of the body with our spiritual life, while seen as radical by the dominant culture, is a natural expression of the way we connect with one another through our physicality: a hug, a conversation, enjoying a meal, making love.

In Zen, we value the body as our dharma container—complex and rich in its capacity to appreciate the myriad sights, scents, sounds, and tastes, together with a delightful sensitivity to touch. Here's Whitman again, taking his own delight in the body:

> The curious sympathy one feels
> when feeling with the hand the naked meat of the body, . . .
> The beauty of the waist, and thence of the hips,
> and thence downward toward the knees, . . .
> The exquisite realization of health;
> O I say these are not the parts and poems of the body only,
> but of the soul,
> O I say now these are the soul!

So often we think of our body as a possession that we can treat however we want. Last spring, I broke a tendon in my foot and had to spend over two months on crutches with a medically fit boot that went well above my ankle. I referred to this as my practice partner: if I took care of it, it would take care of me. And it did. Since getting out of the cast I am definitely more sensitive to and appreciative of my body.

In Zen meditation, a primary focus is on grounding and aligning the body, both on and off the cushion. If you notice that you're continually slumping, you may gently bring yourself to an erect posture, and bring your awareness to any bodily tension or anxiety that arises.

Likewise, if you notice each emotion or sensation as it arises, you have the opportunity to accept each one rather than imposing old patterns that create stiffness and rigidity in both mind and body. Perhaps you'll realize that your body has been carrying the weight of some dissatisfaction. If we see this dissatisfaction in an attentive, nonjudgmental way, our slumping usually corrects itself.

We talk a lot in Zen about the sensations associated with anger, trauma, desire, and hatred. But I've noticed that there's a lot of confusion about our body and our relationship to it, probably left over from our puritanical past. Prohibitive and restrictive ideas about the body do not fit very well within Zen teachings. Bare awareness of our bodily sensations allows us to overcome much of that confusion.

Meditating on the body takes us out of our head. After all, the language of the body is sensation. By turning inward, bringing our awareness to our whole body and its sensations, we become more attuned to a mode of perceiving that is intuitive, centered, and compassionate.

SHIKANTAZA: SUBJECTLESS/ OBJECTLESS MEDITATION

In the godhead there is no trace of God.

—Meister Eckhart

Shikantaza is another type of unfocused meditation. *Shikan* translates to "just" and *taza* is "sitting."

In shikantaza, not only is there no object to focus on, there's also no you. It is the profound realization that the so-called subject—the "I"—is just a conglomeration of ever-changing thoughts and feelings, with no abiding substance at all. Subjectless meditation opens directly to heart-mind. We wake up from our thought-induced trance and realize there is no one who needs to awaken and no one who has awakened.

Shikantaza is the practice of relaxing into don't-know mind. It is the radical realization that we don't know what's going on in the constant flux and flow of life, so there's nothing to do, no one to be.

Early on in my practice, a friend I'll call Luke went to Japan because he wanted to practice at a monastery where he could immerse himself in shikantaza. Luke found just the right place, one that emphasized long periods of shikantaza. However, he didn't realize that he would be there during tourist season, a time when the monastery welcomed and took care of guests. To his dismay, he was sitting even less than we did at our home Zen center in San Francisco because of all the rituals associated with serving guests.

Luke complained to the teacher, reminding him that he had come all this way to practice shikantaza. The teacher responded, "Oh, you misunderstand shikan. It is very important, but it takes many different forms, not only shikan-taza (just sitting) but also shikan-washing dishes and shikan-serving guests—both just as important."

Luke was disappointed, but he did his best to follow the teacher's instructions. One morning, he mistakenly went through the wrong door after breakfast and there was the teacher reading the newspaper in his little alcove, and at the same time listening to the radio and sipping coffee.

Appalled, Luke blurted out, "What are you doing? I thought you said whatever activity I do, just fully give myself to that single activity, so-called *shikan.*"

The teacher replied, "Oh you still have big misunderstanding. Right now, I am reading the paper, drinking coffee, and enjoying music on my headphones—all *shikan.*"

With no mind, flowers lure the
butterfly;
with no mind, the butterfly visits
the blossoms.
Yet when flowers bloom, the butterfly
comes;

when the butterfly comes,
the flowers bloom.
—Ryokan

This poem reminds me of Suzuki Roshi. It was as if everything he did was shikan. Once, I picked Suzuki up at the airport after a trip to Montana. He had been visiting his student Trudy Dixon, the editor of *Zen Mind, Beginner's Mind*, at her parents' ranch. I asked him how he had spent his time. He exclaimed gleefully, "We rode horses!" Puzzled, I said, "I didn't know you knew how to ride horses!" He replied, "I don't know, but the horse knew."

Suzuki Roshi totally imbibed shikan. Shikan riding a horse, shikan playing tennis for the first time, shikan coming to San Francisco and working with a group of counterculture hippies. He embodied don't-know mind.

To get a sense of don't-know mind, you must steep yourself in the practice of subjectless/objectless meditation again and again. You must dip the tea bag into the hot water again and again.

It's quite wonderful when the flavor of the water changes and becomes sweet. This is the taste of stillness. And that sweet stillness bubbles up right in the middle of your churning mind—nowhere else.

ON THIS ROAD WALKS NO ONE

As you develop your meditative practice, you will find that you become more discriminating about what and whom you allow into your life and what you give time and attention to.

As you likely gleaned from what I wrote above about my father's insistence that I become a doctor or lawyer, he strongly opposed the spiritual path I'd chosen, so I had to protect myself from his negative vibes. I disengaged from him during my early years of practice. Then later, when I felt steadier in my practice and life choices and he'd had time to cool off a little from what he viewed as a rejection of his core values, I was able to engage with him again. And this worked out very well.

As you divest yourself of those activities and relationships that do not support your spiritual quest—as I did in my early years of practice—you may experience some loneliness. Even after some years of practice, my loneliness began to creep back up again. As Suzuki Roshi's popularity increased and along with it our membership, the San Francisco Zen Center needed to expand. In 1966, our intimate little practice center purchased a resort in the mountains above Big Sur and converted it into Tassajara Zen Monastery—the first Zen monastery in the United States.

The purchase and development of Tassajara was a big drain on Suzuki's time. Where before I had enjoyed access to him whenever I wanted, I now felt squeezed out by all the people flowing in, whom I saw as interlopers. I was jealous and lonely, and my loneliness and jealousy became major stumbling blocks—so much so that I might have abandoned my practice altogether. But instead, I increased the amount and rigor of my meditation. And then one evening after meditation, I happened to come across a poem by Basho.

> On this road
> walks no one
> this autumn eve.

Suddenly, there was a feeling of being embraced by all of life. I understood with my whole body and mind what Basho was experiencing as he wrote the poem. Even calling it "my experience" doesn't feel quite right. It felt like a direct transmission from Basho's heart-mind to mine—which is also yours.

8

A DOOR BETWEEN
ANY TWO PINES

Between any two pine trees, there is a door leading to a
new way of life.

—John Muir

The Scottish-born American naturalist John Muir (1838–1914),
also known as the Father of the National Parks, was arguably
America's first influential modern environmentalist. Without
John of the Mountains, Yosemite National Park would probably
not exist. He was also influential in the creation of the Grand Canyon, Kings Canyon, Petrified Forest, and Mount Rainer National
Parks. "In every walk with nature one receives far more than he
seeks," wrote Muir. "When one tugs at a single thing in nature,
he finds it attached to the rest of the world."[16]

Twenty-five hundred years before Muir wandered our remot-
est wildernesses and received more than he sought, a man named
Siddhartha, after wandering for seven years, also discovered far
more than he sought when he famously sat down under a bodhi
tree and realized the interconnected nature of the universe.

Following the tradition of pilgrimage, during the height of
Chinese Chan's primacy (seventh–twelfth centuries) monks and

nuns traveled on foot from monastery to monastery, teacher to teacher, relying on the natural world and the teachings of the Buddha to help them return to their original nature. These spiritual seekers were said to "drift like clouds and flow like water."

Still today, mountains and valleys, clouds and water, carry significant symbolic importance in Zen. Whenever possible, monasteries are built on mountains, surrounded by woods and streams. My own students must do a monthlong retreat prior to ordination. Some seek the solitude of a hermitage, others backpack alone deep in the mountains, still others choose a monastery. Like the monks and nuns before them, they rely on the natural world and the teachings of the Buddha to help them return to their original nature. And most often, like the monks and nuns before them, they discover more than they sought.

RETURNING TO THE BONES OF THE EARTH

During the years before the global COVID-19 pandemic, pilgrimage was on the rise worldwide, even while church attendance was in decline. Many people were—and still are—turning to the rawness of nature in search of authentic spiritual experiences, rather than the tired truisms and stale ritual of churches and temples.

To make pilgrimage is to step out from our everyday groove and open our hearts and minds to being reshaped and refreshed by the wilds of the natural world. Almost every summer in my childhood and adolescence, my family backpacked in the Sierra Nevada of California. My father carried a John Muir guide and read aloud from it each evening. Although I didn't realize it at the time, Muir was my first spiritual teacher.

In hikes I've made over my lifetime, whenever I get above the timberline it seems as if I have returned to the bones of the earth, with no hint of how to get where I'm going or what these bare bones will reveal. In many ways, these bare bones of the earth are much like the bare wall in Zen meditation. As we sit, facing the wall, eyes slightly open, hour after hour, day after day on long retreats, we stare at the bare bones of our meditative mind, not knowing where our meditation will take us or what will happen. Following the footprints of the historical Buddha, we learn to stay the course when we encounter the intangible, barren, interior space, with only the occasional cairn to guide us through, not knowing where we're going—until suddenly we awaken to a sense of deep interconnectedness. As the buffers of time and space dissolve, we may cry out joyously, as the Buddha did, "Only I, alone and sacred."

Alone, because nothing within the undivided I is excluded. Sacred, because when everything is sacred, there's nothing that is not sacred, no distinction between the sacred and the mundane.

To experience vidya is to see the bare rock outcroppings that mark timberline, the bare bones of our meditative mind, as guides that lead us back to our roots—to Jizo, the dark, fertile earth womb from which all life comes and to which all life returns.

NOTHING HIDDEN

Our inner life is complete
when it merges into Nature
and becomes one with it.

—D. T. Suzuki

Zen is about experiencing the essence of life directly. That means a direct experience of the natural world beyond what our eyes reveal. The sutras and the myriad texts can point the way, but at some point, we have go beyond the sutras. We have to go beyond a conceptual understanding of the teachings and philosophy. No matter how deep your comprehension may be, it will not match the wisdom that nature—which includes your own Buddha-nature—reveals.

In Zen, all things are dharma, all things are our teachers. But among the myriad dharmas, none are so close to the Dharma as nature itself. When we keenly observe the natural world, we discover that each aspect of it contains its own intelligence and is continually showing us possibilities for action.

When salmon return to their ancestral waters to spawn, they swim upstream and often up waterfalls. To climb a waterfall, the salmon turns the underside of its body into the current. The impact launches the salmon upward through air and water. Over and over again, turning itself toward the impact and accepting it, the salmon makes its way up the waterfall. By observing the salmon, we learn to turn into our difficulties, accept the impact with grace, and through this acceptance and grace, return to our own ancestorial waters.

The journey of the salmon is just one example of how the natural world, which includes all life, is self-emergent and interdependent. Despite apparent conflicts within the plant, animal, and human world, *all* life is governed by an underlying symbiotic relationship, nurtured continuously by the earth womb.

When vidya arises, and our vision pristinely clears, nothing is hidden. When our vision is veiled by greed, hatred, and ignorance—avidya—our mind is not free, and our intrinsic nature is covered over. Even so, vidya—the door to awakening, to wholeness—is closer than you think, closer even than your own breath.

Just outside the walls of a monastery flowed a fast-moving stream. A monk asked, "Where do I enter the path?"

The teacher responded, "Can you hear the sound of the stream?"

"Yes, I can hear it."

"Enter there," the teacher said.

WHOLE AS AN UNCARVED WOODEN BLOCK

The sages of old were fluid as melting ice.

Whole as an uncarved block of wood.

Receptive as a valley.

Turbid as muddied water.

Who can be still until their mud settles

and the water clears by itself?

Can you remain tranquil until right action occurs by itself?

The Master doesn't seek fulfillment.

Only those who are not full are able to be used.

This brings the feeling of completeness.

—Lao Tzu, Tao Te Ching

In the Taoist tradition, Lao Tzu's uncarved block represents our authentic self, our original face—fluid, receptive, sometimes turbid, other times clear, always complete. When we act from this uncarved block, the most ordinary activities become quite extraordinary. We're able to live with a rhythmic ease as our need to be anyone other than who we are vanishes.

Releasing—letting go of our storied experiences, thoughts, judgments—is the key to appreciating the original simplicity of the uncarved block. Each time we rehash an event from the past, a layer is formed that distorts the memory. But when we return to the simplicity of our uncarved block nature, our ability to enjoy life is no longer diminished by past traumas and dramas.

In traditional Buddhism, the effort to let go of our storied experiences, thoughts, and judgments is an example of *jiriki,* meaning "self-power." Through our own effort—whether through bare awareness practice or just being in nature with our whole body and mind—we come to realize that our individual consciousness, our ego, is not separate from our undivided consciousness. The energy that created and sustains our individual self is the same energy that pulsates through our undivided self, and through all life.

Nature never deliberates,
it acts directly out of its own heart,
whatever this may mean.
Nature is divine in this respect.
—D. T. Suzuki

Living from this divine wildness, our thinking becomes flexible enough to plant ourselves deeply in our surroundings, wherever we are and within each difficulty we face. When our thinking mirrors nature, uncalculated and undiluted, we learn to live directly, from our own heart-mind, and to fully embrace our life regardless of what is happening.

Often, we become afraid of anything that appears wild or out of control, even though our body and our world are full of areas that are "wild." These uncontrolled systems regulate themselves quite well. They cooperate, accommodate, and sustain life. The broken tendon in my foot healed itself.

To be whole. To be complete.
Wildness reminds us what it means
to be human, what we are connected
to rather than what we are separate from.
—Terry Tempest Williams

When we are deeply immersed in nature, we witness its unfolding: Trees are inseparable from the parasites that live within them. Worms are inseparable from the birds that eat them. Birds are inseparable from the snakes that eat their eggs. As we witness nature's unfolding, our own grievances begin to dissolve on their own, allowing us to experience the wholeness of Lao Tzu's uncarved wooden block.

NATURE'S WISDOM: THE WOOD WIDE WEB

In the sixth century, Lao Tzu's uncarved wooden block referred to the interconnected wholeness that the natural world continuously manifests. In the twenty-first century, our cutting-edge scientists have made a similar discovery. They call it the Wood Wide Web.

Suzanne Simard, renowned ecologist and author of *Finding the Mother Tree: Discovering the Wisdom of the Forest* (published in 2021), is credited with the discovery that trees all over the world actually communicate with each other through a network of fungal filigrees—latticed fungi buried in the soil.

Another cutting-edge scientist, Merlin Sheldrake, biologist and author of *Entangled Life: How Fungi Make Our Worlds, Change Our Minds, and Shape Our Futures*, wrote, "A dying tree can empty its remaining resources into the web, so it goes to the community. For example, a seedling that is being deprived of sunlight due to a forest canopy will receive resources from the nearby dying tree."[17]

Beyond sharing nutrients and information, through the Wood Wide Web trees search out their kin and sabotage interlopers by spreading toxic chemicals throughout the network. If a tree is being invaded by a predatory insect, it can send out an alert to the community so neighboring plants can raise their defenses. Fungal networks can even boost a host plant's immune system.

Nature's wisdom and power, revealed centuries ago through Lao Tzu's poetic expression of an uncarved block, is today scientifically confirmed and measured. With this a new expression has emerged: the earth's natural internet. In his article "The Secrets of the Wood Wide Web," Robert MacFarlane wrote, "The revelation of the Wood Wide Web's existence, and the increased understanding of its functions, raises big questions—about where species begin and end; about whether a forest might be better imagined as a single superorganism, rather than a grouping of independent individualistic ones; and about what trading, sharing, or even friendship might mean among plants."[18]

DOGEN'S MOUNTAINS AND WATERS

To hear sounds with the whole body and mind,
to see forms with the whole body and mind,
one understands them intimately.

—Dogen

To hear and see a mountain with our whole body and mind is to completely enter the mountain. In Dogen's Mountains and Waters Sutra, he points out that there is no separation between the sutra and the actual mountains and waters. "The mountains and waters *are* the sutra," he proclaims.[19] When you completely enter the mountain, you completely enter his most profound teachings. Referencing this sutra, author and teacher John Daido Loori said, "The appearance of the mountains is completely different when we are in the world gazing at the distant mountains and when we are in the mountains meeting the mountains."[20]

Entering the mountain is about intimacy. When intimacy is present, any notion of *otherness* vanishes. The dichotomy between self and other no longer exists. *You* no longer exist. But that's okay. *You* never existed anyway. You have never been the separate, isolated, and lonely being that you identified with. That is simply how you appear when you gaze at yourself through the lens of your small self. Being "in the mountains meeting the mountains" means you are meeting your true interbeing nature. You have completely entered the mountain.

Earlier, I briefly mentioned my backpacking trips in the Sierra Nevada with my parents. Now I want to share a memory, still vivid all these years later, of my fifth or sixth trip, when I finally fully entered the mountains. I was nine years old.

It was July, just at dawn, when we began our hike to the 14,000-foot peak of Mount Langley. We traveled for several hours up its pine-forested side, and although the trail was steep, reading the trail signs posted at least every quarter mile helped me stay focused and gave me a sense of security. I remember saying to myself each time I saw a sign, "8.8 miles left," "8.6 miles left," "7 miles left . . ."

But when we got to the timberline, the trees vanished, the trail turned into nothing more than an animal track, and there were no more trail signs. Suddenly, I felt disoriented, exhausted, and I wanted to quit. But my mother was up ahead of me, urging me on.

As I followed her slow, steady footsteps, I began to release any thoughts about how far we had come or how far there was still to go. I began to settle into a "one step, one breath" focus. Fear and anxiety dropped away. Immersed in my uncarved block nature, I was able to completely enter the mountain.

Mountains walking are like humans walking.

—Dogen

Suzuki Roshi embodied Dogen's Mountains and Waters Sutra. When he sat in meditation, he sat like a mountain, imperturbable as the traffic rushed by on the busy San Francisco street outside. And yet, when he was not sitting, tenderness, generosity, and compassion flowed like water into everyone he met.

The place where we walk has a way of walking in us. The mountain is the mind and body of the walker, and the walker is the mind and body of the mountain.

—Eido Carney

Dogen tells us to fully enter the mountains and fully enter the swamps. When we do this, we realize that the mountains and swamps are not something out there—they are our own body and mind, and simultaneously our own body and mind are the mountains and swamps.

Sometimes our mind is clear—we are optimistic, spontaneous without being impulsive, our energy is up, and we experience a deep sense of compassion toward everyone. The negative flows right off our backs like water off a duck. We can still feel the inner presence of past traumas and the chattering of monkey mind, but we are not bothered; it's white noise. When we lean into Dogen's mountains and waters, the swamps do not bother us in the least. This is spiritual liberation.

It is only our attachment to the fears and desires of the ego that keeps us from experiencing the mountain's unbroken, nonstop flow. It's important to realize, however, that this unbroken, nonstop flow not only includes the birds and the sky and the stars—things that symbolize freedom and expansion—but also the backwaters and the swamps.

If we can maintain our ability to just be with whatever happens—even as our mind becomes increasingly swampy, constantly pouring over the past and projecting into the future—at some point the pollution settles and an even deeper clarity than before arises.

Doesn't life, and often your own body and mind, sometimes feel like a stagnant, backwater swamp? When my own needy little self raises its swampy head, I remember what Dogen said about it:

There are mountains hidden in treasures.
There are treasures hidden in mountains.
There are mountains hidden in swamps.

There are times when our thoughts are inundated with fear or hate. But there are mountains and streams within that swamp—lessons to learn, inner strength to cultivate, compassion to foster, and unqualified freedom to experience.

Water is nature's purest expression of absolute freedom. Being free of form and formlessness, it can manifest as a river, a swamp, a block of ice, a billowing cloud, as steam, or as condensation. Dogen tells us that water, being free of all dualities, is dependent only on itself:

Water, being dependent on water, is liberated.

The first time I came across this teaching, I was quite confused. But if you think about it, what we perceive always depends on us alone, the one doing the perceiving. For example, if you're a surfer riding the perfect wave, water is the most wonderful thing that ever existed. However, you might have a different experience if you were adrift in a tiny lifeboat and that same perfect wave came barreling across the ocean toward you.

Water's freedom depends only on water in the same way that your freedom depends only on you.

Water is neither strong nor weak,
Neither wet nor dry,
Neither moving nor still,
Neither cold nor hot,
Neither existent nor nonexistent,
Neither deluded nor enlightened.

A student once told me about a dream she'd had. She was a mountain stream, flowing freely, undeterred by stones or fallen trees, going under, over, or around, with uncalculated panoramic awareness. She awakened with an intense feeling of exhilaration. I asked her, "Were you dreaming then, or are you dreaming now?"

A PILGRIMAGE THROUGH NOT-KNOWING TO INTIMACY

To be on pilgrimage is to continue, undeterred by any difficulty or obstacle that comes up. Moment-to-moment nonstop flow applies to all life. Whatever happens, a pilgrim puts one foot in front of the other. Might your difficulties be entirely about your perceptions and expectations rather than the journey itself?

Every spring for the past few years, the mosquitoes have been feasting on my skin during walking meditation in the backyard at our Zen center. Maybe my blood has gotten sour over the years, but I have found that when I just let them do their thing, completely accepting any distress or impatience that comes, they no longer disturb me.

If you follow the river all the way back to its source, there
    are clouds.
If you follow the clouds all the way back to their source,
    there is the river.
—Dogen

Whatever impediment comes up, just continue. Continue to follow the cairns, regardless of how infrequent they become. Continue until there are no cairns at all, and then continue still. "If you want to tame a horse, give it a large pasture." When the pasture of your mind is large enough, you don't know what is over the next hill. Your awareness scans the horizon of your mind with great curiosity. When there is no expectation or desire, our awareness is soft and gentle. This is how we tame intrusive thoughts and return to our source.

A pilgrim said to Master Caoshan, "My name is Qingshui. I am solitary and destitute. Please give me alms."

Caoshan responded, "Venerable Shui!"

"Yes!"

"You've already sipped three glasses of the finest wine in the nation. And yet you say you've not put the cup to your lips."

Qingshui was a student of the wild, a student of intimacy. He may have felt as isolated and alone as I did years ago after two months at Tassajara Zen Monastery when I obsessively counted and recounted my mosquito bites. He may have felt as sorry for himself as I did, but neither of us had anything to complain about. We weren't homeless, hungry, or unsafe. We were surrounded by mountains and waters and enlightened before we were born. So we had already sipped the finest wine.

A feeling of being in total darkness—isolated, bereft, and alone—often precedes awakening. The darkness, the earth womb, has a way of dissolving even our most beloved concepts and ideas and opening our heart and mind to an entirely new reality.

Luckily, Qingshui had a spiritual friend to help him go beyond the limitations of his plaintive cry, a spiritual friend who reminded him, "You've already sipped three glasses of the finest wine in the nation."

If we can learn to rest in the darkness of don't-know mind, our life starts to work effortlessly, as we no longer feel cut off from others or the world around us. If you enter Dogen's mountains and waters, the boundaries that separate and divide will drop away and Dogen himself may meet you there. If you don't see him, perhaps Yangshan can help.

A monk asked Yangshan, "How do you turn mountains, rivers, and the great earth into the self?"

Yangshan replied, "How do you turn the self into mountains, rivers, and the great earth?"

THE SEED OF ENLIGHTENMENT

Once, there was a tiny acorn living on a hilltop overlooking an apple grove. The acorn spent its days gazing in wonder at the beautiful grove down below. It was in awe of these lovely trees, with their green leaves waving in the wind and the plump, red orbs hanging from their branches.

The acorn dreamed about being so tall and full of leaves. "Maybe, if I truly put my mind to it, I could become just like them," the acorn thought.

Day after day, it concentrated. With all its might, it tried to will itself into a beautiful apple tree. It imagined what it must feel like. Sometimes its imagination was so vivid, it could feel itself sprouting branches that moved with the wind. But when it opened its eyes, it was still a tiny acorn. No matter how hard it tried to realize its dream of being an apple tree, it remained an acorn.

"Maybe I should pray," it thought. So it prayed to the sky above and to the earth below. It prayed to the stars at night and to the sun at its highest. It prayed to the rain as it fell, and even to the apple orchard below. It beseeched and pleaded and implored.

Then one day, as it was trying to bargain with the sky, promising to be the best apple tree the sky has ever seen, if only, if only, if only—

"What are you doing?" asked a crow.

"I am praying to the sky."

"What are you praying for?"

The acorn told the crow of its deep desire to become an apple tree like those in the meadow down below. It explained how it had first tried with all its might to will itself into an apple tree, but its efforts had failed. Then it had prayed diligently to the sky and the earth, the stars and the sun, and the rain. But its prayers went unanswered.

"They're lovely alright," said the crow. "But they are apple trees. They grew from apple seeds. You're an acorn. You can pray all you like, but you'll never be an apple tree." Then, using its beak, the crow turned the acorn around.

Suddenly, the tiny acorn was met by the most beautiful tree it had ever seen. It was so tall it almost reached the sky and was filled with so many leaves, the acorn couldn't even see around it. It was magnificent.

"That is your father and your mother, that is your grandparents and your great-grandparents," the crow said. "You are that and it is you."

"I don't understand," said the acorn. "How could that be?"

"It is an oak tree. And its seed is within you."

Look within!

The secret is inside you.

—Huineng

As the little acorn discovered, jiriki alone can only take us so far. But it didn't give up. It turned to the second kind of power from Mahayana Buddhist teachings—*tariki*, "other power." Tariki could be a spiritual community, a mentor, a teacher, or the teachings. Some are inspired by ritual, others by bare awareness meditation or prayer. To the little acorn, tariki meant prayer. It prayed to the sky, to the earth, to the stars, the sun, and rain—but pray as it may, it did not sprout branches with lovely red orbs and green leaves waving in the wind.

Jiriki didn't seem to work; tariki didn't seem to work. But then what happened?

The crow happened.

The crow is the mythological, pitch-black messenger of the gods and the guide into the unknown. Wholehearted effort, whether it is jiriki or tariki, is never fruitless. All the crow did was turn the little acorn around, expanding its view, and its original face was revealed.

9

STUMBLING TOWARD ENLIGHTENMENT

A greatly enlightened person is nevertheless deluded. To understand that is the quintessence of practice.

—Dogen

The stumbling toward enlightenment phase of Zen practice is about learning from our blunders, misunderstandings, doubts, and misgivings. The way we stay engaged in the process is by recognizing and radically accepting when we have gone off course.

Zen teacher Taigen Leighton said, "It's extremely important in practice to make mistakes." Mistakes arise naturally when we embrace don't-know mind. Even though we don't know where we are within the process of awakening, or where we are going, or how to get there, we remain curious. And curiosity is the spark that fires our attention and vitalizes our commitment to the path.

At this stage of practice, we don't even know what we don't know, so in every moment we are open and attentive and we listen deeply to hear the quiet voice behind our loud, chattering monkey mind. And we notice when we're holding to some fixed idea of how it should be. Dogen called this wholehearted engagement "practice-enlightenment" because, to Dogen, each moment of wholehearted practice is a moment of enlightenment.

Don't-know mind allows our brain to expand. Scientists call this neuroplasticity, which means the suppleness and flexibility that our brains and nervous systems retain, to some degree, throughout our lives. When we think we know something, we contract around what we think we know. As our mind fixates on some idea, flexibility is lost. We become brittle. Don't-know mind allows us to just relax into our life.

The aspiration to stay fully engaged in a dynamic and unknowable reality is what Dogen called authentic practice. With don't-know mind, we listen with our whole body and mind. Don't-know mind allows us to see with clarity because our view is not obstructed by our preconceived and often arbitrary ideas.

Dogen's practice enlightenment includes both vidya and avidya, clarity and delusion. When avidya is present and we recognize it as ignorance and let it go—that is vidya. This simple shift in perspective, when repeated again and again over time, gives us insight into the interplay between delusion and enlightenment. This interplay is Dogen's practice enlightenment.

About three years after I began my Zen practice, during a long retreat at Tassajara, I had an enlightenment experience. I was ecstatic and felt radically changed on the deepest level. On my way home, I couldn't wait to show my mother how meditation had transformed me.

But when I walked into the house, she met me with a long, disapproving look. "Don't they feed you at that place?"

I went from ecstasy to anger in ten seconds. Ecstasy this moment, anger the next—moment-to-moment nonstop flow. How wonderful this interplay between enlightenment and delusion—although that's not how I felt at the time.

THE WINDS OF CHAOS AND WISDOM

We should view chaos as very good news. Chaos dissolves all our concepts. It brings us face to face with Reality as it actually is.

—Chögyam Trungpa Rinpoche

The Buddha often warned his followers of the eight opposing energies, called the eight worldly winds—gain and loss, praise and blame, pleasure and pain, happiness and unhappiness. These are the primary bearers of adversity in our life.

The adversity comes when we compulsively chase the former—gain, praise, pleasure, happiness—and work to avoid the latter. Often calling these opposing energies the "terrible twins," the Buddha warned about the futility of that chase—if we cling to one, we cannot escape its opposite.

The terrible twins are not inherently corrupt. A desire to own a nice car or enjoy a delicious meal is fine. Enjoying recognition for a job well done or admiration by others for some achievement is wonderful. The problem arises when we are driven by these desires because we believe that without them, we cannot be happy. It is not the prevalence of the winds that determines whether we'll live a good life or an unhappy one; it is how we handle them when they arrive.

These opposing energies around which we organize our life bring both chaos and the potential for deep wisdom. No matter how advanced your Zen practice may be, you will experience the underlying push/pulls of the worldly winds. However, with practice you learn to work with the energies as they arise. Observing a particular entanglement, you look to see how you identify with it, and you notice how easily you become frustrated and disappointed.

The eight worldly winds point directly to our state of mind. Meditation offers the opportunity to become aware of our mind's contents and to cultivate the ability to free ourselves from what William Blake called "mind-forged manacles." The ability to identify the eight worldly winds enables us to open beyond the imprisonment of our mind-forged manacles and embrace all life, regardless of the direction and prevalence of the wind.

There are many koans and Zen stories about our entanglements with the terrible twins—some are staunch and somber, other humorous. Here's an example of Zen humor:

Two monks, Su Dongpo and Foyin, lived across the river from each other. One day, feeling quite advanced in his Zen practice, Su Dongpo wrote a poem expressing his deep realization and asked the boatman to deliver it to Foyin.

Head bowed to the heaven within
Fine light illuminating the universe
No longer moved
By the eight worldly winds.

Receiving the poem, Foyin wrote a quick response. When the boatman returned bearing Foyin's comment, Su Dongpo, expecting words of praise from the Chan master, quickly opened it.

What he read however was one word: "Fart!"

Upon seeing such an insult, Su Dongpo's anger flared. Immediately, he boarded a boat and crossed the river to confront his old friend.

"How could you insult a dharma friend like this?" he demanded.

"I did not mean to insult you. Did you not say that the eight winds cannot move you? Yet, here you are, blown all the way across the river by a single fart."

EMBRACING OUR FLAWS

The Japanese Zen aesthetic called *wabi-sabi* is about deeply appreciating the natural cycles of life. As a philosophy, wabi-sabi embraces life's imperfections and reveres authenticity. As a practice, it offers a way to live our lives that cultivates joy, compassion, and wisdom.

The first word, *wabi*, is about the beauty of humble simplicity. *Sabi* expresses the splendor of the passage of time, the coming and going of things, including all life. Together, these two concepts create an attitude in which we engage with all of the elements of our experience.

Wabi-sabi has three primary features: imperfection and irregularity, age, and simplicity and naturalness. Zen places a high value on each of these qualities. We find them in pottery, brush painting, the tea ceremony, and poetry, as well as the lives of spiritual adepts within the Zen tradition.

One of the most important aspects of wabi-sabi is opening up to and appreciating our flaws. Often, this includes reaching out to others for support in a way we wouldn't normally risk doing. The recognition that others are flawed in similar ways offers opportunities to develop bonds that are deep and long-lasting. All life has imperfections. Regardless of how good we are at meditation, our shadow side will always be with us, revealing what's hidden so that we can heal.

Someone once complained, after reading my book *Zen in the Age of Anxiety: Wisdom for Navigating Our Modern Lives,* "All your book does is tell me over and over to sit in meditation and accept, accept, accept. How does that help?"

This reader was right—what an imperfect book! And yet, I can't help but feel that he didn't understand that the desire to be in a different state of mind or situation than our current one inhibits our natural flow. When you reject this moment because it is unpleasant, you are rejecting the only moment you have to be alive. And as long as you cling to regret and disappointment about the future or the past, you will not experience the natural flow that Lao Tzu talked about.

Healing begins with embracing our flaws. Compassion begins with embracing the flaws of others. Within the flux and flow, all things are incomplete and imperfect. Wabi-sabi teaches us to embrace, rather than resist, these qualities.

> The master was asked by his followers, "How can you be happy in a world of impermanence?"
>
> The master held up a glass and said, "Someone gave me this glass, and I am quite fond of it. It holds water and tea admirably and glistens in the sunlight. One day the wind may blow it off the shelf, or my elbow may knock it from the table. And I say, 'Of course.' When I understand that the glass is already broken, every moment with it is precious."

DELUSION RECOGNIZED IS ENLIGHTENMENT

In one of his most famous teachings, Dogen wrote, "To study the Buddha way is to study the self." Dogen's "to study the self" is not about an academic or intellectual pursuit. It's not about examining our childhood or asking if we're in the right job, the right relationship, or if we'll ever find happiness. While this approach may get you a better job or a great relationship, it will not lead to enlightenment.

For Dogen, and consequently, in Zen practice, studying the self is about learning to recognize and accept our delusion. A moment of recognition, acceptance, and letting go of our delusion is a moment of enlightenment.

To study the self in this way requires courage, commitment, and a willingness to go into the dark places of our psyche. Our delusions frequently arise from the rejected parts of our personality that operate outside of our awareness.

From our earlier discussion, we know that everyone has endured emotional difficulties that splinter the personality. Bringing these inner fragmentations into the light is the deepest self-study we can do. Healing the divide between self and other begins within, with our own fractured self. Viewed now through the lens of Dogen's practice-enlightenment, we may learn to recognize and even appreciate each fractured aspect of our personality as a guidepost to enlightenment.

Wholeness is the natural state of all beings, and enlightenment is about returning to our natural state. The rejected parts of our personality, our shadow selves, are seeking unification. Reintegration of our shadow self is how we return to our natural state of wholeness.

When we respond to a situation in impulsive and destructive ways, when we are confused about our own actions, when we hurt someone we love out of anger, chances are some shadow from the past is sending us a message that we have a wound here that needs our attention.

Our shadow will allow us no peace without its integration. If we withhold our kind awareness from old wounds, we will continue to be triggered, to act out in chaotic and confusing ways. These repeated patterns can dominate our life. Your shadow self is powerful, and it will not be ignored. It will keep showing up until you're ready to acknowledge its presence and accept it back into your heart. To sponsor your shadow is to mentor it back into the light.

Jack had doubts about his ability to get beyond the mental chatter, chatter, chatter during meditation. I worked with him for a couple of years, helping him to sponsor both his doubts and his chatter. He began by cultivating the ability to look at them with innocent curiosity.

Curiosity is a state of openness. It is inviting and welcoming. As Jack's heart opened, a feeling of lightness flowed in and manifested as a tender presence that allowed him to welcome his doubt, along with the mental chatter that arose from it. As the tender presence surrounded and permeated the doubt, his mind became still for the first time. What began as innocent curiosity culminated in a deep sense of calm, centeredness, and quietude. Jack's meditation was transformed from frustration to peace.

All of us have experiences or behaviors that are neglected, ignored, and shut out of our heart. These neglected or hidden parts of our personality repetitively assert themselves. Each time they are rejected, they manifest in increasingly troublesome and disruptive ways. And each time they're rejected, they become more deeply entrenched within our psyche.

> The damming of life cannot continue forever.
> Sooner or later, the river leaks through,
> bringing with it a myriad of memories, dreams, and
>   reflections.
>
> —Stephen Gilligan

Instead of damming off parts of ourselves, we can bring our fractured self into our meditation, again and again, until we return to our natural state of wholeness. As wholeness returns, our life becomes free of harmful impulses, addictions, and numbness— and free of fake smiles and pretenses.

To study the self in this way is deep work. But that's what Zen is about—it's what this entire book is about. As the dam breaks and the river of life flows freely within us and through us, we may stumble into the realization that each of us, fractured or healed, is included in whole-being Buddha-nature—just as we are.

ENLIGHTENMENT IS AN ACCIDENT

"To study the Buddha way is to study the self," wrote Dogen. "To study the self is to forget the self."

Eventually, if your practice is wholehearted, studying the self begins to raise a sense of dis-ease. Our consciousness created a bounded self because it felt threatened by a hostile world. Being totally surrounded by impenetrable walls feels safe. Both Buddhism and modern science tell us that this cycle of threat and defense is deeply ingrained.

Understandably, the "forgetting the self" stage of Zen practice puts us in a precarious spot. It's where we begin to feel the confinement. What once felt safe and secure begins to feel like a sort of imprisonment.

It's one thing to study the self and to experience the confinement of a separate, isolated self—it's quite another to push up against it. It's a seemingly inscrutable dilemma—the *you* that is struggling for freedom does not exist. And the harder we push against our sense of a separate self, the more it contracts and the more solid it feels.

It's painful to recognize that you're confined to a limited and constricted space. To move through the boundary you have created, first you have to get very close to it and experience your dis-ease directly, without pulling back into your comfort zone. At this phase of practice students often become disoriented. It is meant to be disorienting. The "forgetting the self" stage presents an opportunity to reorient to a world without boundaries.

Once, at a weeklong retreat, a student, whom I'll call Samantha, signed up for a one-to-one meeting with me. When she sat down, she just began to shake her head in despair. "I'm exhausted," she said. "I just can't get it."

I couldn't help but smile. Samantha was right where she was meant to be. She was right where Dogen put her.

I leaned in, pointing my finger at her chest for emphasis, and said, "No, Samantha. You. Can't. Get it."

To study the self is jiriki, self-power. It is a thorough and exhaustive study. And the more exhausted the mind becomes, the less energy it has to push up against something that doesn't exist, that has never existed. I recognized that Samantha was very, very close to realizing her true, undivided self.

When our exhausted mind finally gives up and becomes still, the boundaries that divide and isolate begin to dissolve. It happens on its own; it is tariki, other power. It is the crow, gently turning us inward so we begin to see with the penetrating eyes of vidya.

BECOMING ACCIDENT PRONE

To study the Buddha way is to study the self.
To study the self is to forget the self.
To forget the self is to be enlightened by all life.
To be enlightened by all life is to
free your body and mind and those of others.
No trace of enlightenment remains,
and this traceless enlightenment is continued forever . . .
—Dogen

"To forget the self" is to become accident prone. "To be enlightened by all life" is tariki: your sense of self fades into the background on its own, and your authentic self, your original face, naturally and spontaneously comes forward. When we are enlightened by all things, the most ordinary activities become quite extraordinary. We live with a rhythmic ease as our need to be anyone other than who we are vanishes.

Once, an old man fell into the rapids and was swept over a dangerous waterfall. When he emerged unharmed, onlookers asked him how he survived.

"Without thinking, I allowed myself to be shaped by the water," he said. "Plunging into the swirl, I came out with the swirl."

When the old man fell into the rapids, he completely forgot the self as a separate being. Dogen calls this the dropping away of body and mind. Merging with the swirl, he was enlightened by the swirl. At that moment, his original face was realized, and it was completely ordinary, beyond any trace of being enlightened—or not.

PART THREE

FALLING AWAKE

You've got to bumble forward into the unknown.

—Frank Gehry

10

PENETRATING DUALISTIC THINKING

The whole universe is one bright pearl.
We cannot help but love this one bright pearl
that shines with boundless light.

—Dogen

Dogen's metaphor of one bright pearl includes our very own body and mind. It points to a way of living beyond the limitations of self-centered pleasure-seeking and pain avoidance. It also suggests that we can see through the veil of alienation and isolation affecting so many of us. When we open up to the universe as one bright pearl, we feel centered and whole; we are no longer trapped within habitual and reactive patterns of behavior.

That's not to say we don't need habitual patterns to live a well-balanced life. From the moment of birth and throughout the *selfing* process, patterns will emerge—we need healthy ones to thrive in the world, including those that are self-protective. But when we realize and act from the whole universe as one bright pearl, we are no longer trapped in our patterns. We are free to choose which ones are useful and which no longer serve us.

Even so, not a single thought, emotion, or behavior is separate from Dogen's one bright pearl. Anger, despair, confusion, malaise—all are nothing other than one bright pearl. When we see the pearl of the universe within each moment and *as* each moment, even our tragedies become a portal, a shining beacon in the dark, radiating everything with its warm glow.

COLLAPSING THE DICHOTOMY
BETWEEN SUFFERING AND JOY

To the oyster, the grain of sand that produces a pearl is an unwelcome intruder. The suffering oyster yearns to rid itself of the abrasive stowaway, much the same as we yearn to avoid our own pain. One could argue that avoiding pain is the primary focus of contemporary Americans, but this is not true for all cultures throughout time.

The culture of ancient Greece celebrated the human struggle and suffering. In Homer's *Odyssey,* Odysseus's struggle to return home entailed great suffering, noble suffering, even glorious suffering, which gave his life deep meaning.

This approach to suffering as something to be valued and engaged is important in finding freedom. More than a decade ago, I worked with a student named Helen who was suffering from chronic fatigue. Whereas my family of origin's core value was being smart, her family's core value related to continually working hard. I helped Helen hold in her heart-mind both the value of working hard and the equally important value of deep rest. As she explored both sides with the bright light of awareness, her chronic fatigue gradually diminished and then vanished. In a meeting with me she glowed as she exclaimed, "I can both do great work and relax deeply." What began as an abrasive piece of sand lodged in Helen's unconscious was transformed into something wonderful as the dichotomy between suffering and joy collapsed.

Søren Kierkegaard, the Danish philosopher and writer, was a good example of someone who knew how to collapse the dichotomy between suffering and joy. One of his biographers wrote:

> By the age of 25 he had lost both his parents, and five of his six siblings. In addition to this, his sensitive temperament, his tendencies to melancholy and anxiety, and his difficult relationships to his father and his one-time fiancée Regine gave him an intimate understanding of various kinds of psychological pain. Rather than avoiding or denying suffering, Kierkegaard was unusually willing to confront it and investigate it. His sensitivity to suffering extended to others: one of his friends remembered that "he gave consolation not by covering up sorrow, but by first making one genuinely aware of it, by bringing it to complete clarity."[21]

Like Homer's *Odyssey,* Kierkegaard's struggle entailed great suffering. But his willingness to confront and investigate his suffering gave his life deep meaning.

AVOIDING SUFFERING FLATTENS LIFE

Unfortunately for us—and the oyster—transformation usually involves pain. Fortunately for us, Zen practice reveals the secret to accepting and growing from the curveballs life throws at us, rather than feeling defeated, humiliated, shame, passivity, helplessness, or guilt.

Furthermore, it's a basic principle of Buddhism that it's our *reaction* to painful situations that is a problem. Our strong resistance to pain—and attachment to pleasure—creates a life of suffering.

Resistance to whatever is happening caps off the natural well-spring of energy and creativity that comes with transformation.

So the first step toward creating an unflat life is to cultivate the ability to flow with the ups and downs that arise. For most of us, life brings an equal amount of pain and happiness. Each time we welcome what comes as a guest rather than an intruder—regardless of whether we view it as pain or happiness—we collapse the dichotomy between suffering and joy. We can just rest in the boundless light of one bright pearl.

That's not to say that anyone ever learns to flow through life perfectly. Even advanced practitioners get caught in the web of either/or thinking. But as your meditation matures, you will develop a capacity to acknowledge, and even embrace, all your emotions without judgment. Then, if you have hurt someone with your single-mindedness, you quite naturally apologize and move on without a lot of excuses or resistance.

In chapter 4, I discussed how new practitioners often worry about losing themselves in their quest for spiritual and emotional maturity. They seem to hold some idea that a spiritual person lives a flat and uninteresting life, believing on some level that living without judgment and resistance may become dull and unfulfilling. We often harbor stereotypical ideas about what a spiritual person looks like and how they speak and behave, as if there's a mold that they squeeze themselves into.

We need to be careful not to conflate spirituality and religiosity. Religion often prescribes behavior, asking its adherents to meet specific expectations, while spirituality calls on us to harmonize with the deepest nature of our being. We are spiritual beings by nature, and if we patiently and persistently continue our meditation practice, we fall into our deepest and truest self—curious, energetic, and with a passion for life.

Often, in both self-help and spiritual circles, we hear the

phrase "fake it till you make it," which can be helpful when you're trying to learn something new or embarking on a different career or self-help path. However, in spiritual practice the pretense could morph into spiritual bypassing rather quickly.

I prefer another way. Rather than trying to fake our way through our weaknesses and limitations, we can use our weaknesses and limitations as a psychological map that takes us deeply into our psyche. As we do this, we see ourselves clearly, without judgment or denial, and no longer lose ourselves in pretense or posturing. Instead, our own authentic self emerges quite naturally. I call this process opening through the center of our suffering.

For those walking a spiritual path, the weaknesses and limitations encountered along the way are not obstacles; they are waking places. So rather than trying to "fake it till we make it," we can embrace our emotional and mental difficulties as the shining light of one bright pearl.

Surrender is another key component to collapsing the dichotomy between suffering and joy. I am not talking about surrendering your personal power to a deity or even another person. I am simply talking about surrendering to what is. This type of surrender involves staying present for whatever pain you are feeling, regardless of its emotional power, instead of allowing yourself to be swept away by it.

It takes courage to give your all to something while at the same time letting go of any expectation of gain or fear of loss, but this is what living an awakened life is all about. Basho understood this well when he wrote:

A cicada shell;
it sang itself
utterly away.
—Translation by R. H. Blyth

When we "sing ourselves utterly away," we are free to live moment by moment, with both spontaneity and naturalness, no longer boxed in by conditioned patterns inherited from our parents and our culture. Again, as Suzuki Roshi said, "If you want to tame a horse, give it a large pasture." Within this large pasture, either/or is replaced by both/and.

NAGARJUNA'S FOURFOLD UNDERSTANDING

Any commitment requires that we relinquish something. A commitment to deep spiritual practice is a commitment to the unknown, the unfamiliar. We must be willing to become like the serpent, which, when it casts off its old skin, is no longer armored against the world. It experiences feelings and sensations long suppressed. It sees with new eyes. Life is fresh and filled with possibilities.

The second-century Buddhist sage Nagarjuna, whose name actually means "serpent hero," was a master of skin shedding. According to Buddhist mythology, Nagarjuna earned his name by winning the trust of the nagas, who protected the Buddha's most advanced teachings by hiding them away in an underwater cave for more than four hundred years, waiting for the time when spiritual practitioners were ready to receive them.

Considered the supreme teacher of early Mahayana Buddhism, Nagarjuna had a unique teaching style: through a series of dialectical interactions with his followers, Nagarjuna demolished every limiting belief that was presented to him.

He is best known for the tetralemma, or fourfold understanding, which states that there are four possibilities to any proposition. Huayen master Fazang's golden lion is a good illustration of this method of understanding.

Fazang, who lived in the seventh century, created a lion statue out of gold to demonstrate the freedom and flexibility of nondual thinking. If one contemplates the lion, there is only the lion and the gold is not seen—the gold is hidden, and the lion is manifest. If one contemplates the gold, the lion is hidden, and the gold is manifest. This fourfold understanding, or tetralemma, applied to the statue, looks like this:

1. There is a lion.
2. There is no lion.
3. There is both lion and no lion.
4. There is neither lion nor no lion.

Now for an example closer to home: As I write these words, we are in the midst of a global pandemic. You may be suffering from the social isolation of this pandemic, which seems to be going on forever. The first side of the tetralemma is then, "I am suffering." But if you're single-pointedly engaged in reading this book, at this very moment you have forgotten your suffering, or you wouldn't be able to stay focused on my words. Can you broaden your awareness by realizing that right now you are not suffering?

Broadening your awareness even more, you may notice that your mind is capable of experiencing both suffering and not suffering at the same time. This is an example of radical acceptance.

And finally, since "I am suffering" and "I am not suffering" are simply two thoughts, and thought is only a single component of your greater reality, you are neither suffering nor not suffering. At this point, you are surrounded by infinite possibility!

In this case, the tetralemma may be expressed as follows:

1. I am suffering.
2. I am not suffering.
3. I am suffering and not suffering.
4. I am neither suffering nor not suffering.

When we practice in this way, our awareness naturally becomes more open and spacious. As we learn to undulate with the resilience of a great serpent, we become less likely to get caught by either/or thinking.

DANCING WITH NAGARJUNA'S TETRALEMMA

Yangshan asked Shitou, "I understand the Buddha's teaching. But around here, you just sit in silence. What does this mean?"

Shitou responded, "This way will not do. Not this way will not do. Both this way and not this way will not do. Neither this way nor not this way will not do."

As I was writing this book, I began to experience symptoms of Lyme disease—something I'd contracted many years ago but that had been in remission for a long time. The symptoms came on very fast. One day I was energetically preparing to lead a retreat, to be followed by leading an eight-week fall practice period, and suddenly I had barely enough energy to get out of bed. I was physically and emotionally knocked off my feet—and quite angry about it. But I realized I could approach my problem by dancing within Nagarjuna's tetralemma.

I began the dance by first acknowledging my suffering, both from exhaustion and anger. Then, moving toward the opposite end—not suffering—I aroused a deep feeling of gratitude for this rare opportunity to just rest. Moving into the third step of the dance, I shifted my attention beyond the either/or mode to embrace both suffering and the opportunity to rest. Finally, when I was ready, I moved into the last step, releasing both sides and just being with what is.

Did I do it perfectly? Of course not—opening to all four sides of the tetralemma is beyond any idea we may have of perfection.

More recently, when I taught the tetralemma to a group of students, a couple of them admitted to being somewhat bewildered about the actual practice. I asked them to fully embrace their bewilderment, both physically and mentally. When they did this, I helped them open up to and fully inhabit the clarity of that awareness.

Then I suggested they inhabit both the bewilderment and the clarity together until they were ready to let go of both sides. They were able to experience a complete release in both their bodies and minds. Does this sound too good to be true? If so, here's your opportunity: something that is true is also not true, both true and not true, and neither true nor untrue.

Dancing the tetralemma with sincerity is not an easy practice, particularly when our problems arise from our attachment to a certain identity or social persona we're trying to maintain, both of which come into play in my next story.

Almost no one who attends our Zen center smokes. Some time ago, I mentored a woman who, after meeting with me a half dozen times or so, admitted that she was a secret smoker. She was so dismayed and embarrassed about this habit that she had been hiding it from everyone.

I took her through the tetralemma. First, she opened up to her embarrassment and shame. Then I encouraged her to take the second tetralemma step: imagine the soothing sensations of taking a few deep inhales of a cigarette. She did that and I watched her relax and acknowledge how good it felt.

Then I encouraged her to radically accept both sides, aligning herself with both her desire to stop smoking and her desire for the soothing sensations of a cigarette. Then, without being prompted, she exclaimed, "I both want to give it up and don't want to give it up because it feels so good."

Where she'd been boxed in with her either/or thinking, she now was free to both hate smoking and love it at the same time, moving between the two. I don't know whether she quit smoking, but I do know that she had taken a big step toward resolving the struggle between her idealized self and her shadow self. To fully embrace the dance of Nagarjuna's tetralemma, stepping out of our comfort zone is not only required—it's the whole point.

Understanding Nagarjuna's tetralemma from an intellectual perspective is one thing, but practicing it is quite another. So let's look at one more example to see how the tetralemma can resolve a universal emotion that has caused so much pain for so many: anger.

Whenever you get all twisted up over some slight, real or imagined, begin by fully embracing that anger—not with your storytelling mind but in your body where the anger resides. Stay with that anger until it begins to dissipate, which will happen if you truly let go of the thoughts that are fueling it. Then move into the second phase of the tetralemma and experience fully the calm that arises naturally as the strong emotion subsides.

For most people, the third phase is the most difficult, but try to stay with it. Bring the anger back and hold both the anger and your sense of freedom from it together at the same time. Stay with these two seemingly opposing emotional states until they begin to dissolve on their own.

Finally, let go of both and move into neither being angry nor not being angry. Allow yourself to fully embrace this liberative emotional state and the energy that emanates from it.

Emotions such as anger are not the only cause of our discomfort and suffering—all types of thoughts can cause us pain. Often, it seems as if thoughts slip into our mind fully developed and take over. Working with the tetralemma cultivates mental and emotional flexibility and resilience. Habituated patterns, such as comparing, criticizing, and complaining dissolve as we gently and naturally open up to all aspects of our being.

Working with the tetralemma helps us to stay centered—we still get triggered and react to situations, but after an initial swing we quickly return to our center. Suzuki used the metaphor of a swinging door that always returns to its natural state, ready to respond appropriately to the push and pull of moment-to-moment nonstop flow.

Responding from our center also means that we have no particular interest in either delusion or enlightenment, since we quite naturally move from one to the other, to both, to neither, and to graciously and generously sharing ourselves with others, without any ideas of gain or loss. If you're stuck on the idea of being enlightened, you might try the tetralemma to get unstuck:

I am enlightened.
I am not enlightened.
I am both enlightened and not enlightened.
I am neither enlightened nor not enlightened.

Both teachings—emptiness and the tetralemma—express the same view of reality. And both offer profound insight into the root cause and alleviation of suffering. Please remember that Buddhism differentiates suffering and pain. We will always experience the pain of sickness, old age, and death. However, when we embody our nondual nature, we're more able to endure loss without suffering so much over the trials and tragedies of the conventional world.

Whenever we are fixated on an issue, Nagarjuna's tetralemma has a way of dissolving the either/or fixation by deconstructing every reference point we land on. Even so, Nagarjuna's tetralemma practice is inherently dualistic. Perhaps you believe this is a problem. You may be thinking, *But, Tim, I thought the goal is to penetrate dualistic thinking.*

However, according to Suzuki Roshi, "Dualism is no problem."

DUALISM IS JUST AN EXPRESSION OF NONDUALISM

Dualism refers to seeing and experiencing the world through the lens of self/other, mind/body, inside/outside, thought/being. When we think, *I want to improve my life* or *I want to have a better relationship with others,* that's dualistic thinking. When I want to achieve goals such as these, I do a dualistic practice to try to let go of my defensiveness, self-centeredness, and territoriality so I can just be with others and cultivate connections in a genuine way.

Take meditation, for example. Meditation is a dualistic practice used to still and open our mind. During meditation, over and over, we bring our attention back to the object of focus. Then we go out into the world and put our meditation into action by bringing our attention to each activity, whether we're drinking a glass of water or driving on the freeway. If someone cuts us off on the road and we begin to get angry, we can bring our awareness to our breath and anchor ourselves there so we don't get tossed around by our anger. Or maybe we use a mantra—rather than acting on our anger, we repeat the mantra instead. Whatever is happening, stilling and opening our minds will support us.

We do a dualistic practice with a nondual attitude.

—Suzuki Roshi

Central to all Buddhist teachings is another dualistic practice—cultivating compassion. We do this practice by paying attention to our heart. If someone insults you, you feel it in your heart. Can you have compassion for your own heart and for the person who disrespected you? They are acting out their own suffering, and by doing so they are creating future suffering for themselves and others.

Can you imagine what it may be like for them—what may be causing them to behave badly? Compassion is not a passive emotion. We must aspire to it. We may fall short in the last moment, but we can aspire to it in the next moment.

Cultivating compassion is then, at its core, a dualistic practice because there is me and there is you. I'm paying attention to my own feelings and to your feelings. When I'm angry with someone and working to express my compassion toward them, I focus on our connectedness rather than my anger. Gradually, my heart opens, and I return to a place of peacefulness. It takes willingness and inner strength to do these dualistic practices, but we all have the inner resources we need.

To access these vital inner resources, we need to simplify our life—yet another dualistic practice. Instead of mindlessly adding stuff to our lives, practice mindful consumption. This practice asks, *What do I want to take into my life and my body? What do I want to take into my eyes and ears? What helps me to feel connected? And what makes me feel isolated and different from others?*

I remember my fourth-grade teacher saying something like, "In the future, Americans will only be working fifteen to twenty hours a week because of our material wealth and technology." If only she had been right—but instead of slowing the pace of our lives to enjoy our material wealth, we moved in the other direction.

No matter how much wealth we accumulate, it's never enough. Our culture does not support a simple life. I grew up in what is now Silicon Valley, and I often read about how people there work seventy and eighty hours a week. If they don't, they're considered disloyal to their companies. They're even encouraged not to take their vacations because they look like slackers if they do. It's a badge of honor to work so many hours and neglect other aspects of their life. They are driven by the expectations of others.

Of course, not all Silicon Valley corporations encourage and reward behavior like this, but many do. And we're all affected by this mindset, wherever we live. To simplify our life, we first need to be aware of the shifting tides within our culture and question the direction in which we are being driven.

As we aspire to still our minds, cultivate compassion, and simplify our life, our aspiration supports us—it glues our attention to the present moment and keeps our actions intentional. Yet it's important to understand that aspiring to realize something that we haven't realized is, again, inherently dualistic.

To realize our still nature, we aspire to manifest the stillness that is within each of us. We aspire to free ourselves from the little guy in our head who's always driving us to achieve more, consume more, become someone other than who we are. We also aspire to take care of this small, driven self so we can open our hearts to others who are being hypnotized by a culture that divides us from each other and our world. We aspire to feel our connection with others and to come *from* a place of wholeness.

When we infuse our dualistic practices with a nondual attitude, the boundary between you and me softens. Instead of focusing on becoming more important or clinging to some ideal about becoming kinder and better, we notice how programmed we are to improve ourselves—and then we can return to our inherent wholeness.

Inherent wholeness means that we're nobody, that we never were anybody, that we'll never be anybody. The small separate self that yearns to be a "somebody" is just a mental construct. To realize that what is happening is an interchange of energy and life that is always flowing and changing is to manifest our inherent wholeness. Then we can stop using our inner resources to validate me, me, me. We can stop trying to fit our huge, interconnected life into a small story line.

There will always be stories told about life, but we don't have to carry so much confusion inside about who we are, who we should be, or who we might have been. And there's no need to get attached to our ideas about nondualism. Instead, we can appreciate each of our dualistic activities as an *expression of* nondualism—rather than a *path toward* it.

11

PORTALS INTO
BOUNDLESS LIGHT

Flow with whatever is happening and let your mind be
   free.
Stay centered by accepting whatever you are doing.
This is the ultimate.

—Lao Tzu

Little is known about the sixth-century B.C.E. Chinese philosopher Lao Tzu, the reputed author of the Tao Te Ching. He was a recordkeeper in the court during the Zhou dynasty, and when he tired of life in the morally corrupt court, so the story goes, he dressed as a farmer and rode a water buffalo to the western border of the Chinese Empire.

The border guard recognized him and requested that he write down his philosophy and wisdom before leaving China. Then and there, Lao Tzu sat down and penned the eighty-one short chapters of the Tao Te Ching, the foundational text for Taoism, which, in turn, had a foundational influence on the creation of Chan and then Zen.

If you've practiced Zen or aspired to the wisdom of the Tao, you already know that flowing with each activity works well when things are going our way. When we engage in activities we're good at and we love doing, it's quite natural to fall into a flow state.

But what of the times when things aren't going our way, or we when find ourselves in totally unfamiliar terrain? What happens to flow then? Take, for example, the story of an accomplished young archer who could nock, draw, and loose an arrow in a single fluid motion. He prided himself as the greatest archer in the world—until he heard of a Zen master famous for his skills as an archer. Right then he decided to challenge this renowned archer and prove himself to be the best in the world.

It was a long journey across many mountains and valleys, but finally the young man arrived at the monastery and presented his challenge.

When the time came, the young man stepped forward, nocked his arrow, aimed, loosed, and hit the bull's-eye perfectly. Without hesitation, he followed up with a second arrow, which split the first right down the middle.

The young man promptly turned to the Zen master and asked, "Do you think you can match that?"

The Zen master simply gestured for the young man to follow him. They traversed higher and higher up the mountain until they came to a gorge with a log spanning the distance to the other side.

The Zen master calmly stepped onto the log and advanced to the center of the chasm, where he loaded and loosed his arrow into a tree on the far side of the gorge. Then he calmly returned. Stepping back onto the cliff's edge, he gestured for the young man to take his turn.

The youth stared into the depths of the gorge, trembling uncontrollably. He could not even take the first step onto the log. He looked beseechingly at the older man.

"You have great control over your bow," the Zen master offered kindly. "But little over the mind that lets loose the arrow."

DOGEN'S ACTIONAL UNDERSTANDING

The parable of the archer and the Zen master illustrates what Dogen called "actional understanding." Actional understanding is about moving beyond a mere intellectual understanding; it's about meeting and transforming each activity into moment-to-moment nonstop flow. This distinction is important because it is our activities, not our philosophy, that make us accident prone.

An actional understanding of the six *paramitas* is fundamental to Zen practice. In Sanskrit, *para* translates to "beyond," and *mita* to "that which goes." I often refer to the paramitas as the "gone beyonds." Each gone beyond, when thoroughly penetrated, is a portal into boundless light.

The gone beyonds are comprised of six attitudes and practices that can take us beyond the limitations of conceptual thinking and loosen our hold on the sense of a separate self.

The gone beyonds are:

1. Generosity
2. Morality
3. Patience
4. Effort
5. Meditation
6. Wisdom

The real value of a gone beyond lies in its ability to cut through our conceptual framework and question our reference points. For example, conventional thinking says that generosity is the opposite of stinginess, morality the opposite of immorality, and so on. However, getting caught on either side is a thought distortion that binds us to a dualistic mindset.

The first gone beyond is generosity, or *dana* in Sanskrit. In the Diamond Sutra, the Buddha said, "If bodhisattvas act generously beyond any concept of generosity, their merit will be incalculable." A common, conceptual understanding of generosity is that we should put the needs of others above our own. When we commit to a spiritual practice, it's tempting to fixate on this idea of supporting others at the expense of ourselves. But this dualistic view of generosity is not only a thought distortion, but also a detriment to your mental, emotional, and physical well-being—and therefore, unsustainable. This kind of either/or thinking guarantees you no peace.

Authentic generosity is not about trying to be good or to live up to some ideal. Instead, if we're feeling like we're being stingy, not wanting to extend ourselves to a particular person or share with them, an actional understanding of generosity includes opening up to and being generous to this feeling.

When stinginess arises, there's always an underlying constriction. Most likely, our stinginess comes from one or both of our parents—their fears around not having enough emotional support or material wealth were passed on to us.

In my own case, I was taught early on that deep and enduring happiness was directly related to material wealth. Even though I saw the inadequacy of that belief many years ago, it's still in my unconscious and resurfaces on occasion. I've practiced with it enough that I can embrace the underlying fear that evokes it, allowing the belief to lose its power. You might try practicing with your own stinginess in the same way.

To foster real change, we must always begin with the self. By attending to and mending ourselves first, we become wiser, more open, and more sincerely generous to others. The nondual practice of generosity is about seeing and touching the fear that underpins our emotional or material stinginess. When we're generous to our own need to possess or withdraw by attending to our underlying fears, true generosity bursts forth naturally and spontaneously. It happens on its own.

The second paramita is *sila*, or ethical behavior or morality. We have to be careful with this one, too. Codes of moral behavior change over time and from culture to culture. For example, two hundred years ago, the code of behavior around sexuality for a Zen monk or nun dictated celibacy. Today the code has softened, gradually morphing into "do not abuse sexuality." Still, many Buddhist teachers have fallen short, even in its revised form. Mere adherence to a rule may be quite superficial and not very effective.

Rigid codes of behavior may be well-intentioned and even necessary at times; however, too often they become harmful. When I was a college student, our culture's attitude toward sex outside of marriage was going through a radical change, and not everyone thought that change was good.

Embracing the changing attitudes, my girlfriend (and current wife of over fifty years) and I moved in together in San Francisco. We lived there until the building manager discovered we were not married and told us that sex outside of marriage is immoral and abruptly kicked us out of our apartment. It's pretty hard to imagine that happening in San Francisco—or almost anywhere else in the United States—in the twenty-first century.

When we practice sila as a gone beyond, rather than a code of behavior, a heartfelt feeling of connectedness supplants the need to conform to cultural norms or to even think about being morally superior or inferior to others.

The third paramita is *ksanti*, or patience. The kind of transformation that happens in Zen is usually quite gradual, and it can feel like we're making no progress at all—or even worse, that we're regressing. I can assure you, however, it's not that you're regressing. It's that through your meditation practice, you have become more aware of your chattering mind and the underlying motives behind your actions.

We have layer upon layer of veils that protect us from the rawness of painful losses, traumas, and deep-seated emotions—and paradoxically, the more seasoned we become in our meditation, the more endless these veiled emotions and feelings may seem. As we draw back veil after veil, we are often surprised to realize how needy and insecure we are. Then, when impatience wells up, we can become quite discouraged.

But if we do turtle practice (introduced in chapter 3), we gently allow one veil after another to fall away, directly experiencing whatever painful emotion each may be hiding. When our experience becomes a little too raw, we may retreat into the stillness and protection of our meditative shell until some clarity arises.

Most of us, however, are more like the impatient hare. We are in pain and want to escape or transcend whatever difficulty we are experiencing. That means our authentic practice of patience *must include impatience*. When we're patient with our impatience, we discover that turtle practice is not so difficult.

Effort, or *virya* in Sanskrit, is the fourth paramita. Persistent effort, when practiced as a gone beyond, may be the most important of the paramitas. When we are fully engaged in an activity, we go beyond any idea of making an effort. In Zen, this kind of effort is called "effortless effort."

Effortless effort is not as paradoxical as it may seem. If our effort is wholehearted, we find that our worries and concerns about reaching a particular end will drop away. For example, if I completely give myself to sweeping the floor, I'm able to just be with the back-and-forth rhythm of the broom and the swaying of my body—back and forth, back and forth. Before I know it, the floor is clean. I didn't bother myself with the idea of having a clean floor, and yet it occurred.

> When effort is practiced wholeheartedly,
> it is like a good bonfire that burns itself out completely,
> leaving no trace.
> —Suzuki Roshi

When effort is practiced as a gone beyond, that feeling of effortlessness naturally arises. So effortless effort means we are neither clinging to some failure or success from the past nor holding any expectation about the future—there's no separation between the means and the end, between the path and the destination. When we practice wholeheartedly, we are calmly engaged in *this* moment, then *this* moment, then *this* moment—liberated from the strain of before and after. A good bonfire burns without apparent effort, and yet, look at the heat it continually produces.

The fifth gone beyond is *dhyana*, or meditation. Zen is known as the "meditation school" of Buddhism, and at its core, Zen meditation is about cultivating the type of awareness that leaves nothing out. Too often, however, when an anxious series of thoughts or memories arise during meditation, we become confused or dispirited, and we may create a new story about the anxiety. Then, if we wrap ourselves in that story, we're likely to create even more negative emotions.

When practiced as a gone beyond, meditation invites us to open our heart to our feelings and sensations without a hint of judgment or blame. This is intimacy—an intimacy that naturally opens us to the flux and flow of an ever-changing universe.

The final gone beyond is *prajna*, or wisdom. The Sanskrit word comes from the roots *pra*, meaning "before or preceding," and *jna*, meaning "knowledge." This is not the kind of knowledge obtained through reasoning and inference—which are important—but rather our innate wisdom, the wisdom we were born with. Prajna is transformational wisdom that emanates from our interbeing nature.

Prajna is the foundation from which Buddhism arose and flourished. In the Buddhist creation myth, Siddhartha meditated for six days and nights, penetrated the ignorance of our interbeing nature, and became the Buddha, the awakened one.

The Buddhist creation myth both parallels and contrasts those of other major religions. For example, in the Old Testament, Adam and Eve were exiled from their home due to sinfulness, specifically the original sin of disobedience.

In Buddhism, it is ignorance of our interconnectedness that keeps us exiled from our true home. And instead of Eve, it is the blind grandmother who is responsible for getting us into this mess. (It's interesting to note that in both myths, it's the female who gets blamed for our exile.)

Having lost her original sight into the nature of reality (prajna), the blind grandmother feels isolated and alone, cut off from all other beings. And having lost her connection to her original nature, she feels fearful and threatened on all sides. To alleviate her fear, she attempts to control and dominate the world around her.

When I look around today, I see a lot of blind grandmothers and grandfathers. At the time of this writing, we are entrenched in a global pandemic, and many of us feel isolated, lonely, and threatened. Furthermore, socially, politically, and culturally we are painfully divided into separate tribes. Distrust and even hostility between these tribes is at the highest it's been in my lifetime.

The tribe I belong to feels strongly that racial and social minorities remain burdened by our country's long history of political and economic discrimination and plagued by indignities, large and small, because of the attitudes some have about their culture, beliefs, skin color, or sexual orientation. Another major tribe in our culture fears becoming marginalized in the rapidly changing demographics of the United States.

Prajna is about openness and receptiveness. Instead of feeling threatened by others, perhaps all of us blind grandmothers and grandfathers can follow Lao Tzu's advice to just flow with whatever is happening, allowing our mind to be free.

TAKING THE BACKWARD STEP

Take the backward step and turn your light inwardly to illuminate the self.

—Dogen

In addition to the gone beyonds, another portal into boundless light is Dogen's backward step. When we take the backward step that shines the light inward, all volitional activity stops. So the backward step is quite different from the common approach to meditation.

We generally engage in meditation with a purpose, as with most activities we undertake. Maybe we're trying to quiet our mind, to be free of some emotional trauma, or simply to be more intimate with the world around us.

However, trying to get *anything* from our meditation glues us to the foreground of our mind where all our assumptions about self and other reside. By contrast, Dogen's backward step is about receding into the background of our mind. It happens on its own—any effort to prolong the experience moves you back into the foreground.

Even though volitional activity stops, that doesn't mean that nothing happens. Each time we allow our awareness to sink deeply inward, we touch some place we have never touched before. And once touched, the route has been marked, much like a synaptic pathway in our brain—only this pathway is toward our interbeing nature, our undivided self. In this deep place, there is no sense of a separate self, and therefore no assumptions and no foreground.

> A truth of spiritual life: that there are moments we come to when our thinking is suspended, and when an old knowing has been dropped and the attachment to a new knowing has not yet arisen. That gap is everything.
> —Karen Armstrong

PORTALS INTO SPACIOUSNESS

> Three things cannot be hidden: the sun, the moon, and truth.
> —The Buddha

As we move from childhood into adolescence and then adulthood, we develop patterns of thinking, behaving, and feeling that will define and limit our experience. As these patterns congeal, our sense of a separate self also congeals. While our sense of self has a crucial place in the conventional world, conditioned patterns based on the past produce a limited view of reality.

Emptiness, when thoroughly imbibed, has the potential to create cracks in both our rigid conditioning and our limiting sense of self. It only takes a small crack for a profound realization of reality to seep into our consciousness and change our lives forever.

The Mahayana teaching of emptiness is difficult for Westerners to grasp because, in the West, it carries a negative connotation completely absent in Eastern spiritual teachings. In a Western context, it's used to refer to a sense of joylessness, meaninglessness, and even hopelessness.

Beyond that, the term itself is often used interchangeably as a state of mind, a philosophical view, or a mode of perception. For example, the emptiness of the Taoists refers to a state of mind where all our worries and concerns have dropped away; it's the experience of a deep inner stillness.

The emptiness of Buddhist philosophy, however, points to the illusory nature of reality—the way we see things is not the way they are. As a simple example, consider two of the most basic illusions our brain creates: colors and shapes. What we call red, science calls a light wave with a length of 650 nm and frequency of 4.62×10^{14} Hz. Even though we know we're looking at a light wave of a certain length and frequency, still we see only red.

Shapes, too, have a hidden truth that eludes our mind's eye. All boundaries, no matter how distinct they appear, are fluid, permeable, ever-changing, and their existence is totally dependent on the entire cosmos: atmospheric pressure, temperature, the earth's rotation, the position of the moon, to name a few. Our sense of self, which enables us to survive and get along in the world, is conditioned to divide up our experience based on the way we label it.

Although the emptiness of Buddhist philosophy concerns the nature of reality, the emptiness of Buddhist practice refers to a mode of perception. To perceive emptiness is to be free of the stories we tell ourselves, our strongly held opinions, and our conditioned beliefs.

When you adopt emptiness as a mode of perception, your mental and emotional entanglements begin to dissolve. You see how transparent your emotions are and experience how quickly they disintegrate.

Emptiness as a mode of perception is the cultivation of vidya, deep seeing. And vidya, by its very nature, gives rise to a loosening of our attachments, leaving the mind empty of the conditioned greed, anger, and delusion (the three poisons) that dominate so much of our experience. Jonathan Swift, seventeenth-century essayist, satirist, and cleric, once said that *vision is the ability to see the invisible.*

Cultivating vidya as the ability to see the invisible requires training in virtue, concentration, and discernment. Without this training, the mind persists in false narratives that create suffering for oneself and others.

CULTIVATING THE EMPTY FIELD

In the mind of the twelfth-century Chinese Chan master Hongzhi, emptiness becomes a field of awareness as he urges us to "cultivate the empty field." Hongzhi's empty field is a totally fallow and seemingly barren expanse, and yet it is within this field that all life is germinated, grows, and thrives. In early Buddhist teachings, this is referred to as either Buddha-nature or the Buddha womb from which our very life springs.

To sink into Hongzhi's empty field, we must relinquish our hold on the foreground so we can relax into the background. This is much like the backward step, but with one big exception— cultivating the empty field is a meditative practice in which volitional action is involved.

An expression adopted by Hongzhi to describe the empty field is "silent illumination." Although he didn't coin this beautiful expression, Hongzhi is the one most strongly associated with it. He delved into this expression in his poem "Song of Silent Illumination." It's too long to include here, but this two-line excerpt gives you a taste of its simple eloquence.

In silence, words are forgotten.
In utter clarity, things appear.

Hongzhi's empty field is a quiet, unobtrusive, and unreactive awareness. If we settle into this deep silence, we see each moment clearly and release each thought, and its accompanying emotion, with a liberating clarity. However, if we narrow our focus on the breath or the repetition of a mantra, or use any meditation technique at all, we may feel calm, but it is not with the clarity, openness, and flexibility of the empty field.

The Heart Sutra, the tetralemma, and the empty field teachings are all pointing to a world in which limitations become possibilities. As our sense of a separate self softens and becomes permeable, loneliness and isolation dissolve into a feeling of wholeness and completeness, regardless of what's happening in our lives or in the world. All three teachings encourage us to expand our sense of self to include all reality, so we can manifest both our individual and undivided nature.

LIVING FROM THE EMPTY MIDDLE

Monks, these two extremes ought not to be practiced by one who has gone forth from the household life. There is an addiction to indulgence of sense-pleasures, which is low, coarse, the way of ordinary people, unworthy, and unprofitable; and there is an addiction to self-mortification, which is painful, unworthy, and unprofitable.

—The Buddha

In the above quote, the Buddha is referring to the first middle way, an important teaching carefully articulated in the Pali Canon, one of the first Buddhist texts. It describes the ideal life of a Buddhist practitioner as one of moderation, rather than the extreme of either indulgence or austerity.

The Buddha developed this middle way as a reaction to the indulgence of his youth as a young prince and the extreme austerities that were highly valued by spiritual seekers of his time. During his six years as a seeker, the Buddha practiced many forms of self-mortification, including starving himself.

Enlightenment arose within him only after he gave up these extreme practices. Afterward, he developed and taught what he called the middle way. This early middle way, which included celibacy, wearing discarded rags sewed together as clothing, staying away from money, and not eating after noon, was adhered to by serious meditators—predominantly monks, nuns, and priests—and passed on from generation to generation. However austere it is by contemporary standards, it aided these early practitioners in letting go of their attachment to materiality.

However, the Buddha's middle way was radically different from the middle way that developed five hundred years later in early Mahayana Buddhism. The empty middle way, or the nondual middle way, was articulated clearly by the Buddhist teacher Nagarjuna, whose tetralemma we explored in chapter 10. The basic teaching of the Mahayana middle way is that the division we make between good and bad, up and down, or any set of polarities, is incorrect and somewhat arbitrary, since all life is an inseparable flow of interbeing. Even the so-called "middle" is empty of a separate fixed identity, and consequently it includes all life within it, without distinguishing between the sacred and the mundane everyday world of things.

> Being inseparable from life itself,
> Emptiness cannot be experienced apart from things.
> —Nagarjuna, *Verses from the Center*

The empty middle refers to a place of no fixed ideas, including our ideas about emptiness itself. When we fixate on our aspiration to live from the empty middle, our own aspiration becomes a form of entrapment because it is based on the belief that there is something there on which to fixate.

To experience emptiness is to get a glimpse of the interdependent nature of all that arises. Interdependence means that everything is the cause of everything else and everything is the effect of everything else. Nagarjuna referred to interdependence as the *contingency* of all things, including emptiness itself.

In emphasizing the importance of not separating the sacred from the mundane, the empty middle way becomes a guide for our spiritual quest. As we integrate our whole-body experience of the empty middle, our mind descends into our heart. Then, quite naturally, we embody and bring alive the compassionate wisdom of heart-mind through our words, actions, and interpersonal relations.

Supported by the empty middle, our either/or thinking expands to include both/and possibilities. We feel connected, secure, at peace, and thoroughly integrated with all life. Our life becomes huge—too big to fit into a small sense of self with its limited views and patterned behaviors.

To our rational mind, this sounds like a difficult and complex practice. But to the Zen monk and poet Ryokan, living a simple life in a complex reality is no problem. Imbibe his wonderful teaching and watch your deeply held beliefs dissolve with each passing day.

What was right yesterday
is wrong today.
In what is right today,
how do you know it was not wrong yesterday?
There is no right or wrong,
no predicting gain or loss.
Unable to change their tune,

those who are foolish glue down bridges of a lute.
Those who are wise get to the source
but keep wandering about for long.
Only when you are neither wise nor foolish
can you be called one who has attained the way.

—Zen master Ryokan

12

ENTERING THE UNKNOWN

So you should view this fleeting world—
A star at dawn, a bubble in a stream,
A flash of lightning in a summer cloud,
A flickering lamp, a phantom, and a dream.

—From the Diamond Sutra

The Diamond Sutra is one of the Prajnaparamita Sutras, written at the beginning of the contemporary era. These scriptures create the bedrock for the nondual component of Mahayana Buddhism. Together, they open us up to reality as it is—sometimes referred to as ultimate reality—as opposed to the conventional reality our consciousness creates by dividing things up. Prajna is the realization of emptiness. And the most popular sutra that focuses on emptiness is the Heart Sutra.

IMBIBING THE HEART SUTRA

The Heart Sutra, which is chanted every morning in most Zen centers around the world, challenges our view of reality in a very dramatic way. Perhaps you remember this puzzling and seemingly impenetrable sutra from chapter 3, where it was introduced as the Heart Attack Sutra because it has the potential to demolish our conceptual framework—including our sense of self—leaving only a dynamic process of interbeing.

One reason the Heart Sutra is so difficult to comprehend is that it presents all the teachings of the Prajnaparamita Sutras in a condensed form. Furthermore, it negates the fundamental teachings of the Buddha. To give you a taste of the rhythm and nuances of the Heart Sutra, the following passage was taken from the translation we use at the Minnesota Zen Meditation Center.

> Form does not differ from emptiness, emptiness does not differ from form. Form itself is emptiness, emptiness itself form. Sensations, perceptions, formations, and consciousness are also like this.
>
> All dharmas are marked by emptiness; they neither arise nor cease, are neither defiled nor pure, neither increase nor decrease. Therefore, given emptiness, there is no form, no sensation, no perception, no formation, no consciousness; no eyes, no ears, no nose, no tongue, no body, no mind; no sight, no sound, no smell, no taste, no touch, no object of mind; no realm of sight, no realm of mind consciousness.
>
> There is neither ignorance nor extinction of ignorance, neither old age and death, nor extinction of old age and death; no suffering, no cause, no cessation, no path; no knowledge and no attainment. With nothing to attain, the mind is without hindrance. Without hindrance, there is no fear.

It's quite confusing—and easy to see why some may call it the Heart Attack Sutra. It is also apparent that the Heart Sutra cannot be understood by our logical either/or mind. It's not *meant* to be understood by small mind; it is meant to cut through our dualistic, either/or mind and open us up to a nondual, both/and reality.

It becomes less confusing when we realize that *emptiness* is not a noun; it is a modifier. In other words, emptiness is not a thing—reality is not a thing. Reality, which includes both form and emptiness, is a dynamic process, thoroughly interwoven and thoroughly indivisible.

According to the Heart Sutra, when we experience this dynamic process directly, we are freed from the hindrances—negating yet another key teaching of the Buddha. In our discussion of the hindrances in chapter 4, the Buddha told his followers that we will never be free of the hindrances; they will always come up, so we need to learn to deal with them in a skillful way. So what's going on?

Quite simply, the Buddha is referring to our everyday life in the conventional world, whereas the Heart Sutra is offering a glimpse of the nondual reality that exists beyond conventional reality.

The Heart Sutra continues, "Without hindrance, there is no fear." When our fears are alleviated, so too our suffering, since so much of our suffering is based on fear. But this only happens when we thoroughly digest the teachings of the Heart Sutra, as Keizan did in the following koan.

One night, as the monk Keizan was meditating and hearing the wind whistle past the temple, he had a sudden realization of the nature of reality.

Excited about what he'd realized, Keizan rushed to see his teacher, Master Gikai. "A pitch-black ball soars through the starless night," he exclaimed.

Master Gikai said, "That's good, that's good. But keep sitting, keep sitting."

A few months later, Keizan again went to see his teacher. Gikai, noticing his calm demeanor and clear eyes, said, "Tell me, what have you realized?"

Keizan said, "When it's time for tea, I drink tea; when it's time for rice, I eat rice."

Keizan, who is considered the second founder of Soto Zen in Japan—Dogen being the first—is less well known than Dogen, but one could argue that without Keizan Soto Zen would not have flourished for hundreds of years. Whereas Dogen brought a new level of depth and rigor to Zen practice, Keizan made it accessible to laypeople.

The koan "a pitch-black ball soars through the starless night" is about Keizan's transformation, which happened only after he thoroughly digested his sudden enlightenment. And then, when the teacher again inquired about his realization, with clear eyes and calm composure, he responded, "When it's time for tea, I drink tea; when it's time for rice, I eat rice." This return to the everyday world revealed his whole-body Buddha-nature, which includes both the undivided and individual self. His understanding of form/emptiness had thoroughly penetrated his skin, flesh, bones, and marrow.

The Heart Sutra ends with a mantra: GATE GATE PARAGATE PARASAMGATE BODHI SVAHA. As noted in our discussion of mantra, the first part translates to "Gone, gone, gone beyond, gone completely beyond." *Bodhi* translates to "awake"; *svaha* is an exclamation of joy or ecstasy, expressing what we experience when we thoroughly imbibe this teaching and return to our original wholeness.

INDRA'S NET, THE PIVOT OF NOTHINGNESS, AND WALKING ON THE OCEAN FLOOR

In traditional Buddhist mythology, Indra, often depicted with four arms and riding a white elephant, is the king of the gods. In the realm of Indra, so the story goes, hangs a vast net that stretches out infinitely in all directions. At each node is a mirrorlike jewel that reflects all other jewels in the net. Each jewel contains within it the reflection of every other jewel, so when one is touched by joy or tragedy, all are affected.

This sense of interbeing and connectedness is reflected in the story of the missionary group that went to the Australian Outback to aid the First Nations peoples who lived there. Upon arrival they were met by one of the tribal elders, a very old and very wise woman. She stepped forth and said, "If you are here to help us, don't waste your time. But if you're here because you know that your well-being depends on our well-being, let's get to work."

Both the ancient metaphor of Indra's net and this contemporary story of tribal wisdom beautifully illustrate the interpenetration of all phenomena and the transcendent wisdom that lies at the core of each jewel. In Buddhism, this transcendent wisdom is referred to as our *basic goodness*. It is a fundamental quality rooted in the interbeing nature of reality.

Each of us is a jewel in Indra's net. Each molecule of your being radiates vibrancy and is complete just as it is. Every pore in your body, regardless of how polluted you think the pore is, reflects the entire universe. Each pore is sealed within the nodes of Indra's net, just as it is, both divided and undivided.

The wisdom of Indra's net is always revealing itself to us— from within and without. From within, mirror neurons in our brain connect us to the world, allowing us to learn from others and feel empathy and compassion. From without, we may see the entirety of Indra's net in a tiny dewdrop as it reflects its surroundings, and we see it in the mirrorlike surface of the ocean on a calm day.

On a calm, still morning, the colors of sunrise spill out across the surface of the ocean. As the little sparrow hovers over it, the ocean seals his existence just as he is. He doesn't have to try to be an eagle; he doesn't have to wish he were a dove or a hawk.

The sparrow is completely and authentically itself—and it is the entire ocean.

No matter what happens, you are present in each jewel, whole and complete, just as you are—your authenticity, flaws and all, sealed within the whole. Moment after moment, you experience a vivaciousness that is continually emanating from your Buddha-nature.

Katagiri Roshi often referred to this profound and transformational realization as the pivot of nothingness. From the pivot of nothingness everything arises: anger, fear, heartache, disappointment, confusion. But if we rest in the pivot, we don't resist them, and they don't persist. From the pivot of nothingness, prajna—your basic goodness—blooms in the heart of each jewel, moment by moment.

> The pivot of nothingness is the moment when the life force energy of the universe turns in its direction from emptiness toward the creation of form. Emptiness is not a negation of existence. It represents the vast ground from which everything takes form.
>
> —Andrea Martin[22]

The pivot of nothingness is none other than the timeless present moment where there's no separation between the past, present, and future. It's where your whole-being Buddha-nature is manifest. As Dogen put it, "To swim on the ocean surface while walking on the ocean floor is to manifest your whole-being Buddha-nature."

The surface is the conventional world, the everyday world, which includes our stories, memories, hopes for the future; it is the world of duality, of time, of self/other. The ocean floor is that timeless place of emptiness from which everything arises.

Each crest and trough has its own unique nature, and it also has the nature of the entire ocean—a wave is not separate from the ocean. When riding a crest, we experience exhilaration, joy, and a deep connection with the entire ocean. In the troughs, you learn to trust, to have courage, and to be patient. Surfing on stormy days isn't easy, but the storm is not separate from the calm down below.

Using the techniques introduced in chapter 7, we discover that we don't need to protect ourselves from the moods and nuances of life's great ocean. As we befriend the great unknown and allow its salt water to seep into our pores, we discover that we have the ability to stay right with it in placid times and in turbulent times.

Just as the ocean surface is not separate from the ocean floor, so too the conventional world is not separate from the timeless, undivided reality from which all forms arise and eventually return.

WHEN OUR SENSORY CUES GO DARK

Each time you stay present with fear and uncertainty, you're letting go of a habitual way of finding security and comfort.
—Pema Chödrön

Our sensory cues, which are intrinsically dualistic by nature and function, split reality in much the same way a rainbow splits light. They evolved to orient us to a dualistic world, providing the illusion of safety, security, and comfort in a world of uncertainty.

We need our sensory cues to survive. However, if we remain stuck within the limitations of our mind and seven senses, we will not get a taste of the mysterious unknown where all discriminations fall away.

The seven categories of sensory cues are:

- Visual cues
- Auditory cues
- Tactile cues
- Olfactory cues
- Gustatory cues
- Proprioception
- Conceptual cues

We may feel safer in the world experienced through our seven senses. After all, fear of the unknown is our oldest and deepest fear. Nevertheless, to fear the unknown is to fear our undivided self, our Buddha-nature. An attachment to our sensory cues, especially our conceptual cues, can glue us to our small self and the dualistic world.

Each time you experience an aspect of the great mystery, fear of the unknown arises to pull you back into the security and comfort of your conditioned self. The only way to alleviate that fear is to make friends with it and let go of the security of your sensory cues.

Befriending your fear of the unknown is not about making the unknown known. It is about cultivating the ability to rest in the radical comfort of not knowing that is so incredibly engaging. That wonderful feeling of engagement is the intimacy that arises from our original nondual consciousness.

It is coming home.

True wildness is a love of nature,
a delight in silence, a voice free
to say spontaneous things,
and an exuberant curiosity in the face
of the unknown.
—Robert Bly[23]

ENDARKENMENT:
THE SOURCE OF CREATION

> Te-shan visited Zen master Lung-tan and spent the evening asking question after question. Finally, Lung-tan said, "The night is getting old. Why don't you retire?"
>
> Te-shan bowed and opened the screen to go out. He hesitated. "It is very dark outside," he said.
>
> Lung-tan offered him a lighted candle to guide his way. But just as Te-shan received it, Lung-tan blew it out.
>
> At that moment, Te-shan became enlightened.[24]
>
> —Case 28, *The Gateless Gate*

About twenty years ago, my wife and I went to India to meet the extended family of our son's fiancée. While in a rural part of India, I passed a temple where people were prayerfully calling on Amma and Ma in a pleading and heartfelt manner.

Amma and *Ma* translate to "mother" in both Sanskrit and Hindi. This "mother" refers to the dark mother Kali, the Great Primordial Mother from whose womb the universe is born. The Sanskrit word for the womb or matrix of all life is *tathagata-garbha*. It is totally dark, but from it all light emanates. So the dark mother Kali is also the great mother Prajnaparamita, the mother of all buddhas, and in Taoism, which is naturalistic, she is "the valley of the world."

Mother Kali is the manifestation of chaos and destruction, as well as inspiration and creativity; she destroys and creates. She understands that old ideas, judgments, and habits must be destroyed to make room for the new. And most of the time, old habits die hard. So the dark mother has to be fierce. And she is!

Depictions of Kali are fearsome. Her pitch-black color symbolizes the great mystery—that aspect of reality that is not only unknown, but unknowable. And since the greatest fear of human beings is the unknown, her formidable portrayal matches her role and function perfectly.

It follows then that the most intimate and profound understanding of nonduality is the realization that enlightenment and endarkenment are thoroughly intertwined. Just as enlightenment surrounds and infuses everything, so too does endarkenment. Zen teacher and author Joan Sutherland said, enlightenment is "a marriage of wisdom and compassion, and both wisdom and compassion are made up of enlightenment and endarkenment."[25] Ever since my trip to India, where I first heard the heartfelt pleas to the great Amma, whenever my mind clouds over with fear or worry, I repeat her name over and over until some clarity of mind returns.

Whereas enlightenment is often associated with masculine energy, endarkenment is associated with the feminine, the birther. From its rich fecundity, endarkenment manifests in our subconscious as a muse of creativity, inspiring us to birth something wonderful into the world.

Light is the source of life.
Darkness is the source of Creation.
—Sadhguru Satsang

WITHERING INTO ENLIGHTENMENT

Though leaves are many, the root is one;
Through all the lying days of my youth
I swayed my leaves and flowers in the sun;
Now I may wither into the truth.
—W. B. Yeats, "The Coming of Wisdom with Time"

When my parents took me on that hiking trip in the Sierra Nevada, I remember my nine-year-old self being gripped by fear. We started out before dawn, and gazing up at the 14,000-foot peak of Mount Langley, I wondered, *How can I make such a steep climb?*

When my mother gave me a map of the trail, I held it in my fist like a lifeline. I put all my trust in the map. As long as we followed the map, I thought, we would be okay.

Then we reached timberline and the map ended. There were no more landmarks to mark off. Nothing but barren rocks and the occasional stunted tree, as far as the eye could see.

We often have the same experience in spiritual practice. We learn some basic meditation techniques, like following our breath or repeating a mantra—but at some point, we reach the timberline—lost, disoriented, and engulfed in darkness.

My mother stayed just far enough ahead of me to remain within sight—just as Suzuki Roshi did when I practiced with him. If I lagged too far behind, I ran the risk of getting lost, both on the mountain and in my practice.

So I kept moving—one breath, one step.

The path to the unknown is filled with twists and turns, barren rocks, foul swamps, and fog so thick we can't see where our next step leads. What do we do when we lose sight of the path, or faith in our ability to walk it?

We keep moving—one breath, one step.

When we cling to what worked for us in the past, we are like the Irish poet W. B. Yeats, swaying our leaves and flowers in the sun. At a late stage of his life, however, his ability to create wonderful worlds and insightful poetry deserted him. In his poem "The Circus Animals' Desertion" he wrote, "I sought a theme and sought for it in vain."

What worked for Yeats in his youth, the well-honed tricks of his trade—his map—no longer served him. As with serious meditators, he was stripped of all he'd trusted and identified with.

But he kept moving. He fumbled around until the fog lifted and clarity returned. He moved beyond his familiar patterns, and a new path, authentic and raw, opened up before him.

To uncover our own authentic path, we too must strip away our conditioned way of being in the world and "lay bare all the lying days" of youth. This painful process is like peeling away the layers of an onion—you may despair as you continue layer after layer, but the deeper you peel, the closer you come to the empty center and your true resting place.

After Yeats did his own peeling away, he wrote, in "The Circus Animals' Desertion":

Now that my ladder's gone
I must lie down where all the ladders start,
in the foul rag and bone shop of the heart.

When we finally trust the process enough to rest in the "foul rag and bone shop of the heart," a single ray of light may be all we need to enter the unknown. Regardless of how difficult the moment seems, we take *one breath, one step* until—when we least expect it—we wither into enlightenment.

EPILOGUE
Perfectly Flawed and Enlightenment-Prone

A monk on a pilgrimage decided to visit a sacred mountain monastery with a renowned teacher and a stone bridge famed for its aesthetic uniqueness and functionality. Master Zhaozhou, he had heard, was a teacher of extraordinary power and presence. So beloved was he that the locals renamed the famous bridge the "Stone Bridge of Zhaozhou."

The monk had to travel across great distances. When he finally arrived, he was very disappointed. First, Master Zhaozhou was an unimpressive, shriveled up, ordinary-looking old man. Second, instead of seeing a remarkable stone bridge, he saw only a set of stepping-stones scattered across a stream.

The monk said to Master Zhaozhou, "The stone bridge of Zhaozhou is widely renowned, but coming here I find only a set of stepping-stones."

Zhaozhou said, "You see only the stepping-stones and do not see the stone bridge."

"What is the stone bridge?"

Zhaozhou said, "It lets donkeys cross over and horses cross over."

Zhaozhou was one of the most famous pilgrims of the golden age of Chinese Zen. He was eighty when he finally settled into his small nondescript temple next to the famous bridge.

The monk, like most of us when we encounter a great teacher, received more than he sought. Zhaozhou's gentle response conveyed both compassion for the monk's disappointment and offered insight into the root cause of his pain. Unfortunately, like many of us, the monk was not yet ready to receive the wisdom that he yearned for.

Consequently, he was unable to appreciate the simplicity of the bridge and the careful placement of the stones that allowed not only humans to easily pass, but horses and donkeys also—all while honoring the beauty and wildness of the mountain and the unaffected simplicity of the way.

We, also, are on a pilgrimage, and we often trip over our ideas and judgments about teachers and bridges. Driven by our ideals about the appearance of things, we miss the natural simplicity and authentic practice that each Zen center offers: each is a bridge that allows people of all backgrounds and ethnicities to cross over to the other shore, the shore of awakening.

I often compare our little Zen center in Minneapolis to a rock tumbler. Over and over, we bump up against a myriad of diverse personalities and belief systems until our heart opens and our rough edges become smooth. Even so, those new to practice who come in looking for the perfect place and perfect teacher see only rocks and rough edges—and miss the wonderful transformations that are happening right under their noses.

Suzuki frequently reminded us that in Zen there is nothing special. On good days, you may meditate in perfect posture— nothing special. Other days, you may struggle through the entire meditation session—nothing special. Perfect posture fades. Struggle evokes compassion.

So do not cling to perfect, do not cling to struggle, and do not cling to your ideas about teachers and bridges. Instead, practice "nothing special," and perhaps you will see the original face of Zhaozhou in the unimpressive, shriveled up, ordinary-looking person who is your own teacher.

Long before Zhaozhou became a teacher of extraordinary power and presence, sought after by many for his wisdom, he, too, was a struggling young monk yearning for some special state of mind. Like most of us, he had to be reminded to practice "nothing special."

> Zhaozhou asked his teacher Nanquan, "What is the Way?"
>
> Nanquan said, "Ordinary mind is the way."
>
> Zhaozhou asked, "How do I accomplish ordinary mind?"
>
> Nanquan answered, "You cannot accomplish it with effort. You cannot accomplish it without effort."

You cannot accomplish it with effort because ordinary mind arises on its own. You cannot accomplish it without effort because ordinary mind includes both our dualistic, either/or mind and our nondual, both/and mind.

Rather than ignoring one side while embracing the other, we allow both sides to inform each moment. Enlightenment makes room for our delusions, even while penetrating each delusive thought with our gentle light of awareness. Continuously shedding light on our delusions without blame or criticism, is the most important aspect of an awakened life.

Before he became the Buddha, Siddhartha Gautama, believing the path to awakening meant rejecting his individual self, spent years attending only to his undivided self, and he suffered greatly. It was only after he sat under a bodhi tree for six days, focusing his kind awareness on his individual self—on his desires, his lust, his anger, his greed—that his mind, which had been such a tyrant, finally descended into his heart, its true home, and thereafter he lived an awakened life.

Enlightenment, then, includes the ability to move seamlessly between our dualistic self and our nondual self. In the beginning, it may require continuous effort. Over time, however, as we get into the flux and flow of it, the effort feels effortless—much like a surfer riding the waves. It takes effort to ride the waves; but oh, how effortless it feels!

Riding the waves of the great ocean of life evokes a wonderful feeling of intimacy with all beings, allowing us to sink down into our authentic Buddha-nature, where heart and mind are united.

Centuries after the Buddha's awakening, Dogen stressed the nonseparation between the Buddha's wakefulness and the wakefulness that embraces all life. He coined the term "whole-being Buddha-nature" to evoke the sense that awakeness is not just psychological or spiritual—it includes all life as one undivided interbeing. That means that whole-being Buddha-nature is the very nature of our existence, the fundamental nature of all beings.

Thich Nhat Hanh gave us a delightful way of visualizing our whole-being Buddha-nature:

> If a wave only sees its form, with its beginning and end, it will be afraid of birth and death. But if the wave sees that it is water and identifies itself with the water, then it will be emancipated from birth and death. Each wave is born and is going to die, but the water is free from birth and death.[26]

As spiritual seekers—pilgrims on an inward path—we stay the course, urged on by our longing to awaken, until our heart is pierced and we fall into our intrinsic whole-being Buddha-nature.

There's a famous story that evokes a sense of our intrinsic enlightened nature, our original face, which existed before we were even born, and from which we were never exiled. It is the true story of a golden Buddha famously revealed in 1957. And it feels like a fitting way to end our journey together.

For hundreds of years, a clay statue of the Buddha sat in Wat Traimit in Bangkok. It was almost ten feet tall and weighed 5.5 tons. The monks who carved the statue were tragically murdered when the Burmese army invaded the temple, and so the story of the statue's origin was lost.

In 1957, a decision was made to relocate the temple. As they were moving the clay Buddha, one of the monks noticed a large crack in the clay—and from it emanated a golden light. He ran to get a hammer and chisel and began to chip away at the clay. To everyone's amazement, hidden beneath the clay exterior was a statue of the Buddha made of solid gold.

The story of the golden Buddha is also your story, and my story. It is Siddhartha Gautama's story. And the story of Nanquan and Zhaozhou and Dogen and Suzuki and Thich Nhat Hanh. If they can live an awakened life and act from that golden stillness that's within each of us—so can I.

And so can you.

NOTES

1. Quoted in Tina Fossella, "Human Nature, Buddha Nature: An interview with John Welwood," *Tricycle: The Buddhist Review* (Spring 2011), https://tricycle.org/magazine/human -nature-buddha-nature.

2. Barbara O'Brien, "Buddhists Don't Have to Be Nice: Avoiding Idiot Compassion," *Rethinking Religion*, February 21, 2017, https://rethinkingreligion-book.info/buddhists-dont-have-to -be-nice-avoiding-idiot-compassion.

3. James Ford, "Deep in Poop: Reflections on a Zen Koan," *Patheos: Monkey Mind* (June 2018), https://www.patheos.com /blogs/monkeymind/2018/06/deep-in-poop-reflections-on-a -zen-koan.html.

4. Lewis Carroll, *Alice's Adventures in Wonderland* (New York: Macmillan, 1920).

5. Debra Flics, "What Meditation Can't Cure," *Lion's Roar*, October 24, 2021, lionsroar.com/what-meditation-cant-cure.

6. Taigen Dan Leighton, *Faces of Compassion: Classic Bodhisattva Archetypes and Their Modern Expression—An Introduction to Mahayana Buddhism* (Wisdom, 2012, 2nd ed.), 277.

7. Mark Nepo, *The Exquisite Risk: Daring to Live an Authentic Life* (New York: Three Rivers Press, 2006).

8. "Watching the Moon," in *The Ink Dark Moon: Love Poems by Ono No Komachi and Izumi Shikibu, Women of the Ancient Court of Japan*, translated by Jane Hirshfield with Mariko Aratani (New York: Vintage Books, 1990).

9. Quoted in Susan Moran, "The Science Behind Finding Your Mantra—And How to Practice It Daily," *Yoga Journal*, March 20, 2018, https://www.yogajournal.com/yoga-101 /mantras-101-the-science-behind-finding-your-mantra-and -how-to-practice-it.

10. Rozalyn Simon, Johan Pihlsgård, Ulrika Berglind et al., "Mantra Meditation Suppression of Default Mode Beyond an Active Task: A Pilot Study," *Journal of Cognitive Enhancement* 1, (2017): 219–27, https://doi.org/10.1007/s41465-017-0028-1.

11. Anna Barton, *Tennyson's Name: Identity and Responsibility in the Poetry of Alfred Lord Tennyson* (Aldershot, England: Ashgate, 2008), 13.

12. Zachiah Murray, "How to Do Gatha Practice," *Lion's Roar*, July 25, 2022, https://www.lionsroar.com/how-to-practice -gathas/.

13. Charlotte Joko Beck, "Our Substitute Life," in Lenore Friedman and Susan Moon, eds., *Being Bodies: Buddhist Women on the Paradox of Embodiment* (Boston: Shambhala, 1997).

14. Ryūichi Abé and Peter Haskel, trans., *Great Fool: Zen Master Ryōkan—Poems, Letters, and Other Writings* (Honolulu: University of Hawaii Press, 1996), 75.

15. Walt Whitman, "I Sing the Body Electric," in *Leaves of Grass* (London: Penguin Classics, 2017).

16. John Muir, *John of the Mountains* (Boston: Houghton Mifflin, 1938).

17. Merlin Sheldrake, *Entangled Life: How Fungi Make Our Worlds, Change Our Minds and Shape Our Futures* (New York: Random House, 2020).

18. Robert MacFarlane, "The Secrets of the Wood Wide Web," *The New Yorker*, August 7, 2016, https://www.newyorker.com/tech/annals-of-technology/the-secrets-of-the-wood-wide-web.

19. This quote, and the subsequent quotes from this sutra, are adapted from Dogen, "Mountains and Waters Sutra," in *Treasury of the True Dharma Eye: Zen Master Dogen's* Shobo Genzo, trans. Kazuaki Tanahashi (Boston: Shambhala, 2013), 154–64.

20. John Daido Loori, "Becoming the Mountains and Rivers," *Lion's Roar*, September 4, 2017, https://www.lionsroar.com/becoming-the-mountains-and-rivers.

21. Joakim Garff, *Søren Kierkegaard: A Biography* (New Jersey: Princeton University Press, 2014).

22. Andrea Martin is the editor of Katagiri's *Each Moment Is the Universe* and *The Light That Shines through Infinity.* She was his personal attendant until his death in 1990.

23. From https://minnesotamensconference.com/robertbly, accessed January 24, 2023.

24. Robert Aitken, *The Gateless Barrier* (New York: Farrar, Straus and Giroux, 1991), 208.

25. Joan Sutherland, "Everything Is Enlightenment," *Lion's Roar* (September 27, 2022), https://www.lionsroar.com/everything-is-enlightenment/.

26. Thich Nhat Hanh, *Awakening of the Heart: Essential Buddhist Sutras and Commentaries* (Berkeley, CA: Parallax Press), 426.

INDEX